Gettysburg

Gettysburg

Edited by
CHARLES K. FOX

South Brunswick and New York: A. S. Barnes and Co.
London: Thomas Yoseloff Ltd

A. S. Barnes and Co., Inc.
Cranbury, New Jersey 08512

Thomas Yoseloff Ltd
108 New Bond Street
London, England

SBN 498–06967–2 (cloth)
SBN 498–07446–3 (paper)
Printed in the United States of America

1–12–79

Editor's Preface

There was published in the 1880's a series of four great source books of the Civil War encompassing vivid accounts by eye witnesses of and participants in the most vital and spectacular events. *Battles and Leaders of the Civil War,* reprinted by Thomas Yoseloff in 1960, was a successful editorial concept to record history in the most accurate and entertaining manner. Commanders, subordinate officers and others were induced to participate. A total of 230 contributed.

Gettysburg correlates some of these sterling accounts encompassing: Lee's invasion of Pennsylvania, famous reportings of the three-day Battle of Gettysburg, and Confederate retreat to the Potomac and home soil.

Contents

Gettysburg

The First Day

by Major General Henry J. Hunt, U.S.A.

At 8 A.M., July 1st, Buford's scouts reported Heth's advance on the Cashtown road, when Gamble's brigade formed on McPherson's Ridge, from the Fairfield Road to the railroad cut; one section of Calef's battery A, 2nd United States, near the left of his line, the other two across the Chambersburg or Cashtown Pike. Devin formed his disposable squadrons from Gamble's right toward Oak Hill, from which he had afterward to transfer them to the north of the town to meet Ewell. As Heth advanced, he threw Archer's brigade to the right, Davis's to the left of the Cashtown pike, with Pettigrew's and Brockenbrough's brigades in support. The Confederates advanced skirmishing heavily with Buford's dismounted troopers. Calef's battery, engaging double the number of its own guns, was served with an efficiency worthy of its former reputation as "Duncan's battery" in the Mexican War, and so enabled the cavalry to hold their long line for two hours. When

Buford's report of the enemy's advance reached Reynolds, the latter, ordering Doubleday and Howard to follow, hastened toward Gettysburg with Wadsworth's small division and Hall's 2nd Maine battery. As he approached he heard the sound of battle, and directing the troops to cross the fields toward the firing, galloped himself to the seminary, met Buford there, and both rode to the front, where the cavalry, dismounted, were gallantly holding their ground against heavy odds. After viewing the field, he sent back to hasten up Howard, and as the enemy's main line was now advancing to the attack, directed Doubleday, who had arrived in advance of his division, to look to the Fairfield Road, sent Cutler with three of his five regiments north of the railroad cut, posted the other two under Colonel Fowler, of the 14th New York, south of the pike, and replaced Calef's battery by Hall's, thus relieving the cavalry. Cutler's line was hardly formed when it was struck by Davis's Confederate brigade on its front and right flank, whereupon Wadsworth, to save it, ordered it to fall back to Seminary Ridge. This order not reaching the 147th New York, its gallant major, Harney, held that regiment to its position until, having lost half its numbers, the order to retire was repeated. Hall's battery was now imperiled, and it withdrew by sections, fighting at close canister range and suffering severely. Fowler thereupon changed his front to face Davis's brigade, which held the cut, and with Dawes's 6th Wisconsin—sent by Doubleday to aid the 147th New York—charged and drove Davis from the field. The Confederate brigade suffered severely, losing all its field officers but two, and a large proportion of its men killed and captured, being disabled for further effective service that day. In the meantime Archer's Confederate brigade had occupied McPherson's Wood, and as the regiments of Meredith's "Iron Brigade" came up, they were sent forward by Doubleday, who fully recognized the importance of the position, to dislodge Archer. At the entrance of the wood they found Reynolds in person, and, animated by his presence, rushed to the charge, struck successive heavy blows, outflanked and turned the enemy's right, captured General Archer and a large portion of his brigade, and pursued the remainder across Willoughby Run. Wadsworth's small division had thus won decided successes against superior numbers, but it was at grievous cost to the army and the country, for Reynolds, while directing the operations, was killed in the wood by a sharpshooter. It was not, however, until by his promptitude and gallantry he had determined the decisive field of the war, and had opened brilliantly a battle which required three days of hard fighting to close with a victory. To him may be applied in a wider sense than in its original one, Napier's happy eulogium on Ridge: "No man died on that field with more glory than he, yet many died, and there was much glory."

After the repulse of Davis and Archer, Heth's division was formed in line mostly south of the Cashtown Pike, with Pender's in second line, Pegram's and McIntosh's artillery (nine batteries) occupying all the commanding positions west of Willoughby Run. Doubleday reestablished his former lines, Meredith holding McPherson's Wood. Soon after, Rowley's and Robinson's divisions (two brigades each) and the four remaining batteries of the corps arrived. Rowley's division was thrown forward, Stone's brigade to the interval between Meredith and Cutler, and Biddle's with Cooper's battery to occupy the ridge between the wood and the Fairfield road. Reynolds' battery replaced Hall's, and Calef's rejoined Gamble's cavalry, now in reserve. Robinson's division was halted near the base of Seminary Ridge. By this time, near noon, General Howard arrived, assumed command, and directed General Schurz, commanding the Eleventh Corps, to prolong Doubleday's line toward Oak Hill with Schimmelfennig's and Barlow's divisions and three batteries, and to post Steinwehr's division and two batteries on Cemetery Hill, as a rallying point. By 1 o'clock, when this corps was arriving, Buford had reported Ewell's approach by the Heidlersburg road, and Howard called on Sickles at Emmitsburg and Slocum at Two Taverns for aid, to which both these officers promptly responded. It was now no longer a question of prolonging Doubleday's line, but of protecting it against Ewell whilst engaged in front with Hill. Schurz's two divisions, hardly 6,000 effectives, accordingly formed line on the open plain half a mile north of the town. They were too weak to cover the ground, and a wide interval was left between the two corps, covered only by the fire of Dilger's and Wheeler's batteries (ten guns) posted behind it.

That morning, whilst on the march to Cashtown, Ewell received Hill's notice that his corps was advancing to Gettysburg, upon which he turned the heads of his own columns to that point. Reporting the change by a staff officer to General Lee, Ewell was instructed that if the Federals were in force at Gettysburg a general battle was not to be brought on until the rest of the army was up. Approaching Gettysburg, Rodes, guided by the sounds of battle, followed the prolongation of Seminary Ridge; Iverson's, Daniel's, and Ramseur's brigades on the western, O'Neal's and Doles's on the eastern slope. Ewell, recognizing the importance of Oak Hill, ordered it to be occupied by Carter's artillery battalion, which immediately opened on both the Federal corps, enfilading Doubleday's

line. This caused Wadsworth again to withdraw Cutler to
Seminary Ridge, and Reynolds's battery was posted near
McPherson's house, under partial cover. Stone therefore
placed two of his three regiments on the Cashtown Pike,
so as to face Oak Hill. This left an interval between Stone
and Cutler, through which Cooper and Reynolds could
fire with effect, and gave to these lines a cross fire on troops
entering the angle between them. Robinson now sent his
two brigades to strengthen Cutler's right. They took post
behind the stone walls of a field, Paul's brigade facing west,
Baxter's north. Rodes, regarding this advance as a menace,
gave orders at 2:30 P.M. to attack. Iverson, sweeping round
to his left, engaged Paul, who prolonged Cutler's line, and
O'Neal attacked Baxter. The repulse of O'Neal soon enabled Baxter to turn upon Iverson. Cutler also attacked
him in flank, and after losing 500 men killed and wounded,
3 of Iverson's regiments surrendered. General Robinson
reports the capture of 1,000 prisoners and 3 colors; General Paul was severely wounded, losing both eyes. Meanwhile Daniel's brigade advanced directly on Stone, who
maintained his lines against this attack and also Brockenbrough's of Hill's corps, but was soon severely wounded.
Colonel Wister, who succeeded him, met the same fate,
and Colonel Dana took command of the brigade. Ramseur, who followed Daniel, by a conversion to the left,
now faced Robinson and Cutler with his own brigade,
the remnant of Iverson's, and one regiment of O'Neal's,
his right connecting with Daniel's left, and the fighting
became hot. East of the ridge, Doles's brigade had been
held in observation, but about 3:30 P.M., on the advance
of Early, he sent his skirmishers forward and drove those
of Devin, who had gallantly held the enemy's advance in
check with his dismounted troopers, from their line and

its hillock on Rock Creek. Barlow, considering this an eligible position for his own right, advanced his division, supported by Wilkeson's battery, and seized it. This made it necessary for Schurz to advance a brigade of Schimmel-fennig's division to connect with Barlow, thus lengthening his already too extended line.

The arrival of Early's division had by this time brought an overwhelming force on the flank and rear of the Eleventh Corps. On the east of Rock Creek, Jones's artillery battalion, within easy range, enfiladed its whole line and took it in reverse, while the brigades of Gordon, Hays, and Avery in line, with Smith's in reserve, advanced about 4 P.M. upon Barlow's position, Doles, of Rodes's division, connecting with Gordon. An obstinate and bloody contest ensued, in which Barlow was desperately wounded, Wilkeson killed, and the whole corps forced back to its original line, on which, with the aid of Coster's brigade and Heckman's battery, drawn from Cemetery Hill, Schurz endeavored to rally it and cover the town. The fighting here was well sustained, but the Confederate force was overpowering in numbers, and the troops retreated to Cemetery Hill, Ewell entering the town about 4:30 P.M. These retrograde movements had uncovered the flank of the First Corps and made its right untenable.

Meanwhile, that corps had been heavily engaged along its whole line; for, on the approach of Rodes, Hill attacked with both his divisions. There were thus opposed to the single disconnected Federal line south of the Cashtown Pike two solid Confederate ones which outflanked their left a quarter of a mile or more. Biddle's small command, less than a thousand men, after a severe contest, was gradually forced back. In McPherson's Wood and beyond, Meredith's and Dana's brigades repeatedly repulsed their assailants, but as Biddle's retirement uncovered their left, they too fell back to successive positions from which they inflicted heavy losses, until finally all three reached the foot of Seminary Ridge, where Colonel Wainwright, commanding the corps artillery, had planted twelve guns south of the Cashtown Pike, with Stewart's battery, manned in part by men of the Iron Brigade, north of it. Buford had already thrown half of Gamble's dismounted men south of the Fairfield Road. Heth's division had suffered so severely that Pender's had passed to its front, thus bringing fresh troops to bear on the exhausted Federal line.

It was about 4 P.M. when the whole Confederate line advanced to the final attack. On their right Gamble held Lane's brigade for some time in check, Perrin's and Scales' suffered severely, and Scales' was broken up, for Stewart, swinging half his guns, under Lieutenant Davison, upon the Cashtown Pike, raked it. The whole corps being now heavily pressed and its right uncovered, Doubleday gave the order to fall back to Cemetery Hill, which was effected in comparatively good order, the rear, covered by the 7th Wisconsin, turning when necessary to check pursuit. Colonel Wainwright, mistaking the order, had clung with his artillery to Seminary Hill until, seeing the infantry retreating to the town, he moved his batteries down the Cashtown Pike until lapped on both sides by the enemy's skirmishers, at close range, when they were compelled to abandon one gun on the road, all its horses being killed. The Eleventh Corps also left a disabled gun on the field. Of the troops who passed through the town, many, principally men of the Eleventh Corps, got entangled in the streets, lost their way, and were captured.

On ascending Cemetery Hill, the retreating troops found Steinwehr's division in position covered by stone fences on the slopes, and occupying by their skirmishers the houses in front of their line. As they arrived they were formed, the Eleventh Corps on the right, the First Corps on the left of Steinwehr. As the batteries came up, they were well posted by Colonels Wainwright and Osborn, and soon a formidable array of artillery was ready to cover with its fire all the approaches. Buford assembled his command on the plain west of Cemetery Hill, covering the left flank and presenting a firm front to any attempt at pursuit. The First Corps found a small reenforcement awaiting it, in the 7th Indiana, part of the train escort, which brought up nearly five hundred fresh men. Wadsworth met them and led them to Culp's Hill, where, under direction of Captain Pattison of that regiment, a defensive line was marked out. Their brigade (Cutler's) soon joined them; wood and stone were plentiful, and soon the right of the line was solidly established.

Nor was there wanting other assurance to the men who had fought so long that their sacrifices had not been in vain. As they reached the hill they were received by General Hancock, who arrived just as they were coming up from the town, under orders from General Meade to assume the command. His person was well known; his presence inspired confidence, and it implied also the near approach of his army corps. He ordered Wadsworth at once to Culp's Hill to secure that important position, and aided by Howard, by Warren who had also just arrived from headquarters, and by others, at strong line, well flanked, was soon formed.

General Lee, who from Seminary Hill had witnessed the final attack, sent Colonel Long, of his staff, a competent officer of sound judgment, to examine the position, and directed Ewell to carry it if practicable, renewing, however, his previous warning to avoid bringing on a general engagement until the army was all up. Both Ewell, who was making some preparations with a view to attack, and Long found the position a formidable one, strongly occupied and not accessible to artillery fire. Ewell's men were indeed in no condition for an immediate assault. Of Rodes's 8,000, nearly 3,000 were *hors de combat*. Early had lost over 500, and had but two brigades disposable, the other two having been sent on the report of the advance of Federal troops, probably the Twelfth Corps, then near by, to watch the York Road. Hill's two divisions had been very roughly handled, and had lost heavily, and he withdrew them to Seminary Hill as Ewell entered the town, leaving the latter with not more than 8,000 men to secure the town and the prisoners. Ewell's absent division was expected soon, but it did not arrive until near sunset, when the Twelfth Corps and Stannard's Vermont brigade were also up, and the Third Corps was arriving. In fact an assault by the Confederates was not practicable before 5:30 P.M., and after that the position was perfectly secure. For the first time that day the Federals had the advantage of position, and sufficient troops and artillery to occupy it, and Ewell would not have been justified in attacking without the positive orders of Lee, who was present, and wisely abstained from giving them.

2

The Second Day

by Major General Henry J. Hunt, U.S.A.

As our troops came up they were assigned to places on the line: the Twelfth Corps, General A. S. Williams—*vice* Slocum, commanding the right wing—to Culp's Hill, on Wadsworth's right; Second Corps to Cemetery Ridge, Hays's and Gibbon's divisions, from Ziegler's to the clump of trees, Caldwell's to the short ridge to its left and rear. This ridge had been occupied by the Third Corps, which was now directed to prolong Caldwell's line to Round Top, relieving Geary's division, which had been stationed during the night on the extreme left, with two regiments at the base of Little Round Top. The Fifth Corps was placed in reserve near the Rock Creek crossing of the Baltimore Pike; the Artillery Reserve and its large trains were parked in a central position on a crossroad from the Baltimore Pike to the Taneytown Road; Buford's cavalry, except Merritt's brigade (then at Emmitsburg), was near Round Top, from which point it was ordered that morning to Westminster, thus uncovering our left flank; Kilpatrick's and Gregg's divisions were well out on the right flank, from which, after a brush with Stuart on the evening of the 2nd, Kilpatrick was sent next morning to replace Buford, Merritt being also ordered up to our left.

The morning was a busy one, and in some respects an anxious one; it was believed that the whole Confederate Army was assembled, that it was equal if not superior to our own in numbers, and that the battle would commence before our troops were up. There was a gap in Slocum's line awaiting a division of infantry, and as some demonstrations of Ewell about daylight indicated an immediate attack at that point, I had to draw batteries from other parts of the line, for the Artillery Reserve was just then starting from Taneytown, to cover it until it could be properly filled. Still there was no hostile movement of the enemy, and General Meade directed Slocum to hold himself in readiness to attack Ewell with the Fifth and Twelfth, as soon as the Sixth Corps should arrive. After an examination Slocum reported the ground as unfavorable, in which Warren concurred and advised against an attack there. The project was then abandoned, and Meade postponed all offensive operations until the enemy's intentions should be more clearly developed. In the meantime he took precautionary measures. It was clearly now to his advantage to fight the battle where he was, and he had some apprehension that Lee would attempt to turn his flank and threaten his communications—just what Longstreet had been advising. In this case it might be necessary to fall back to the Pipe Creek line, if possible, or else to follow Lee's movement into the open country. In either case, or in that of a forced withdrawal, prudence dictated that arrangements should be made in advance, and General Meade gave instructions for examining the roads and communications, and to draw up an order of movement, which General Butterfield, the chief-of-staff, seems to have considered an order absolute for the withdrawal of the army without a battle.

These instructions must have been given early in the morning, for General Butterfield states that it was on his arrival from Taneytown, which place he left at daylight. An order was drawn up accordingly, given to the adjutant general, and perhaps prepared for issue in case of necessity to corps commanders; but it was not recorded nor issued, nor even a copy of it preserved. General Meade declared that he never contemplated the issue of such an order unless contingencies made it necessary; and his acts and dispatches during the day were in accordance with his statement. There is one circumstance pertaining to my own duties which to my mind is conclusive, and I relate it because it may have contributed to the idea that General Meade intended to withdraw from Gettysburg. He came to me that morning before the Artillery Reserve had arrived, and, therefore, about the time that the order was in course of preparation, and informed me that one of the army corps had left its whole artillery ammunition train behind it, and that others were also deficient, notwithstanding his orders on that subject. He was very much disturbed, and feared that, taking into account the large expenditure of the preceding day by the First and Eleventh corps, there would not be sufficient to carry us through the battle. This was not the first nor the last time that I was called upon to meet deficiencies under such circumstances, and I was, therefore, prepared for this, having directed General Tyler, commanding the Artillery Reserve, whatever else he might leave behind, to bring up every round of ammunition in his trains, and I knew he would not fail me. Moreover, I had previously, on my own responsibility, and unknown to General Hooker, formed a special ammunition column attached to the Artillery Reserve, carrying 20 rounds per gun, over and above the authorized amount, for every gun in the army, in order to meet such emergencies. I was, therefore, able to assure General Meade that there would be enough ammunition for the battle, but none for idle cannonades, the besetting sin of some of our commanders. He was much relieved, and expressed his satisfaction. Now, had he had at this time any intention of withdrawing the army, the first thing to get rid of would have been this Artillery Reserve and its large trains, which were then blocking the roads in our rear; and he would surely have told me of it.

Still, with the exception of occasional cannonading, and some skirmishing near the Peach Orchard, the quiet remained unbroken, although Lee had determined upon an early attack on our left. He says in his detailed report that our line extended "upon the high ground along the Emmitsburg Road, with a steep ridge (Cemetery) in rear, which was also occupied"; and in a previous "outline" report he says: "In front of General Longstreet the enemy held a position (salient angle at the Peach Orchard) from which, if he could be driven, it was thought our artillery could be used to advantage in assailing the more elevated ground beyond, and thus enable us to gain the crest of the ridge." It would appear from this that General Lee mistook the few troops on the Peach Orchard ridge in the morning for our main line, and that by taking it and sweeping up the Emmitsburg Road under cover of his batteries, he expected to "roll up" our lines to Cemetery Hill. That would be an "oblique order of battle," in

which the attacking line, formed obliquely to its oppo-
nent, marches directly forward, constantly breaking in
the *end* of his enemy's line and gaining his rear. General
Longstreet was ordered to form the divisions of Hood and
McLaws on Anderson's right, so as to envelop our left
and drive it in. These divisions were only three miles off
at daylight, and moved early, but there was great delay in
forming them for battle, owing principally to the absence
of Law's brigade, for which it would have been well to
substitute Anderson's fresh division, which could have
been replaced by Pettigrew's, then in reserve. There seems
to have been no good reason why the attack should not
have been made by 8 or 9 A.M. at the latest, when the
Federal Third Corps was not yet all up, nor Crawford's
division, nor the Artillery Reserve, nor the Sixth Corps,
and our lines were still very incomplete. This is one of
the cheap criticisms after all the facts on both sides are
known; but it is apt for its purpose, as it shows how great
a risk Meade took in abandoning his Pipe Creek line for
Gettysburg on the chances of Lee's army not yet being
assembled; and also, that there was no lack of boldness
and decision on Meade's part. Indeed, his course, from
the hour that he took command, had been marked by
these qualities.

A suggestive incident is worth recording here. In the
course of my inspection of the lines that morning, while
passing along Culp's Hill, I found the men hard at work
intrenching, and in such fine spirits as at once to attract
attention. One of them finally dropped his work, and,
approaching me, inquired if the reports just received were
true. On asking what he referred to, he replied that twice
word had been passed along the line that General Mc-

Clellan had been assigned to the command of the army, and the second time it was added that he was on the way to the field and might soon be expected. He continued, "The boys are all jubilant over it, for they know that if *he* takes command everything will go right." I have been told recently by the commander of a Fifth Corps battery that during the forced march of the preceding night the same report ran through that corps, excited great enthusiasm amongst the men, and renewed their vigor. It was probably from this corps—just arrived—that the report had spread along the line.

On my return to headquarters from this inspection General Meade told me that General Sickles, then with him, wished me to examine a new line, as he thought that assigned to him was not a good one, especially that he could not use his artillery there. I had been as far as Round Top that morning, and had noticed the unfavorable character of the ground, and, therefore, I accompanied Sickles direct to the Peach Orchard, where he pointed out the ridges, already described, as his proposed line. They commanded all the ground behind, as well as in front of them, and together constituted a favorable position for *the enemy* to hold. This was one good reason for our taking possession of it. It would, it is true, in our hands present a salient angle, which generally exposes both its sides to enfilade fires; but here the ridges were so high that each would serve as a "traverse" for the other, and reduce that evil to a minimum. On the other hand it would so greatly lengthen our line, which in any case must rest on Round Top, and connect with the left of the Second Corps, as to require a larger force than the Third Corps alone to hold it, and it would be difficult to occupy and strengthen the angle if the enemy already held the wood in its front. At my insistence General Sickles ordered a reconnaissance to ascertain if the wood was occupied.

About this time a cannonade was opened on Cemetery Hill, which indicated an attack there, and as I had examined the Emmitsburg Ridge, I said I would not await the result of the reconnaissance but return to headquarters by way of Round Top, and examine that part of the proposed line. As I was leaving, General Sickles asked me if he should move forward his corps. I answered, "Not on my authority; I will report to General Meade for his instructions." I had not reached the wheat field when a sharp rattle of musketry showed that the enemy held the wood in front of the Peach Orchard angle.

As I rode back a view from that direction showed how much farther Peach Orchard was to the front of the direct line than it appeared from the orchard itself. In fact there was a third line between them, which appeared, as seen from the orchard, to be continuous with Cemetery Ridge, but was nearly 600 yards in front of it. This is the open ground east of Plum Run already described, and which may be called the Plum Run line. Its left where it crosses the run abuts rather on Devil's Den than Round Top; it was commanded by the much higher Peach Orchard crests, and was therefore not an eligible line to occupy, although it became of importance during the battle.

As to the other two lines, the choice between them would depend on circumstances. The direct short line through the woods, and including the Round Tops, could be occupied, intrenched, and made impregnable to a front attack. But, like that of Culp's Hill, it would be a purely defensive one, from which, owing to the nature of the ground and the enemy's commanding position on the ridges at the angle, an advance in force would be impracticable. The salient line proposed by General Sickles, although much longer, afforded excellent positions for our artillery; its occupation would cramp the movements of the enemy, bring us nearer his lines, and afford us facilities for taking the offensive. It was in my judgment tactically the better line of the two, provided it were strongly occupied, for it was the only one on the field from which we could have passed from the defensive to the offensive with a prospect of decisive results. But General Meade had not, until the arrival of the Sixth Corps, a sufficient number of troops at his disposal to risk such an extension of his lines; it would have required both the Third and the Fifth corps, and left him without any reserve. Had he known that Lee's attack would be postponed until 4 P.M., he might have occupied this line in the morning; but he did not know this, expected an attack at any moment, and, in view of the vast interests involved, adopted a defensive policy, and ordered the occupation of the *safe* line. In taking risks, it would not be for his army alone, but also for Philadelphia, Baltimore, and Washington. Gettysburg was not a good strategical position for us, and the circumstances under which our army was assembled limited us tactically to a strictly defensive battle. But even a strictly defensive battle gained here would be, in its results, almost as valuable as an offensive one with a brilliant victory, since it would necessarily be decisive as to both the campaign and the invasion, and its moral effect abroad and at home, North and South, would be of vast importance in a political as well as a military sense. The additional risks of an offensive battle were out of all proportion to the prospective gains. The decision then to fight a defensive rather than an offensive battle, to look rather to solid than to brilliant results, was wise.

After finishing my examination I returned to headquarters and briefly reported to General Meade that the proposed line was a good one in itself, that it offered favorable positions for artillery, but that its relations to other lines were such that I could not advise it, and suggested that he examine it himself before ordering its occupation. He nodded assent, and I proceeded to Cemetery Hill.

The cannonade there still continued; it had been commenced by the enemy, and was accompanied by some movements of troops toward our right. As soon as I saw that it would lead to nothing serious, I returned direct to the Peach Orchard, knowing that its occupation would require large reenforcements of artillery. I was here met by Captain Randolph, the corps chief of artillery, who informed me that he had been ordered to place his batteries on the new line. Seeing Generals Meade and Sickles, not far off, in conversation, and supposing that General Meade had consented to the occupation, I sent at once to the reserve for more artillery, and authorized other general officers to draw on the same source. This large reserve, organized by the wise forethought of General McClellan, sometimes threatened with destruction, and once actually broken up, was often, as at Malvern Hill, and now at Gettysburg, an invaluable resource in the time of greatest need. . . .

When I arrived Birney's division was already posted on the crest, from Devil's Den to the Peach Orchard, and along the Emmitsburg Road, Ward's brigade on the left, Graham's at the angle, De Trobriand's connecting them by a thin line. Humphreys' division was on Graham's right, near the Emmitsburg Road, Carr's brigade in the front line, about the Smith house, Brewster's in second line. Burling's with the exception of Sewell's 5th New Jersey Regiment, then in skirmish order at the front, was sent to reenforce Birney. Seeley's battery, at first posted on the right, was soon after sent to the left of the Smith house, and replaced on the right by Turnbull's from the Artillery Reserve. Randolph had ordered Smith's battery, 4th New York, to the rocky hill at the Devil's Den; Winslow's to the wheat field. He had placed Clark on the crest looking south, and his own ("E," 1st Rhode Island) near the angle facing west. The whole corps was, however, too weak to cover the ground, and it was too late for Meade to withdraw it. Sykes's Fifth Corps had already been ordered up and was momentarily expected. As soon as fire opened, which was just as he arrived on the ground, General Meade also sent for Caldwell's division from Cemetery Ridge, and a division of the Twelfth Corps from Culp's, and soon after for troops from the Sixth Corps. McGilvery's artillery brigade soon arrived from the reserve, and Bigelow's, Phillips's, Hart's, Ames's, and Thompson's batteries had been ordered into position on the crests, when the enemy opened from a long line of guns, stretching down to the crossing of the Emmitsburg Pike. Smith's position at Devil's Den gave him a favorable oblique fire on a part of this line, and as he did not reply I proceeded to the Den. . . . On climbing to the summit, I found that Smith had just got his guns, one by one, over the rocks and chasms, into an excellent position. After pointing out to me the advancing lines of the enemy, he opened, and very effectively. Many guns were immediately turned on him, relieving so far the rest of the line. Telling him that he would probably lose his battery, I left to seek infantry supports, very doubtful if I would find my horse, for the storm of shell bursting over the place was enough to drive any animal wild. . . . However, my horse was safe, I mounted, and in the busy excitement that followed almost forgot my scare.

It was not until about 4 P.M. that Longstreet got his two divisions into position in two lines, McLaws' on the right of Anderson's division of Hill's corps, and opposite the Peach Orchard; Hood's on the extreme Confederate right and crossing the Emmitsburg Road. Hood had been ordered, keeping his left on that road, to break in the end of our line, supposed to be at the orchard; but perceiving that our left was "refused" (bent back toward Devil's Den) , and noticing the importance of Round Top, he suggested to Longstreet that the latter be turned and attacked. The reply was that General Lee's orders were to attack along the Emmitsburg Road. Again Hood sent his message and received the same reply, notwithstanding which he directed Law's brigade upon Round Top, in which movement a portion of Robertson's brigade joined; the rest of the division was thrown upon Devil's Den and the ridge between it and the Peach Orchard. The first assaults were repulsed, but after hard fighting, McLaws' division being also advanced, toward 6 o'clock the angle was broken in, after a resolute defense and with great loss on both sides. In the meantime three of Anderson's brigades were advancing on Humphreys' and the latter received orders from Birney, now in command of the corps (Sickles having been severely wounded soon after 6 o'clock near the Trostle house) , to throw back his left, form an oblique line in his rear, and connect with the right of Birney's division, then retiring. The junction was not effected, and Humphreys, greatly outnumbered, slowly and skillfully fell back to Cemetery

Ridge, Gibbon sending two regiments and Brown's Rhode Island battery to his support. But the enemy was strong and covered the whole Second Corps front, now greatly weakened by detachments. Wilcox's, Perry's, and Wright's Confederate brigade pressed up to the ridge, outflanking Humphreys' right and left, and Wright broke through our line and seized the guns in his front, but was soon driven out, and not being supported they all fell back, about dusk, under a heavy artillery fire.

As soon as Longstreet's attack commenced, General Warren was sent by General Meade to see to the condition of the extreme left. The duty could not have been intrusted to better hands. Passing along the lines he found Little Round Top, the key of the position, unoccupied except by a signal station. The enemy at the time lay concealed, awaiting the signal for assault, when a shot fired in their direction caused a sudden movement on their part which, by the gleam of reflected sunlight from their bayonets, revealed their long lines outflanking the position. Fully comprehending the imminent danger, Warren sent to General Meade for a division. The enemy was already advancing when, noticing the approach of the Fifth Corps, Warren rode to meet it, caused Weed's and Vincent's brigades and Hazlett's battery to be detached from the latter and hurried them to the summit. The passage of the six guns through the roadless woods and amongst the rocks was marvelous. Under ordinary circumstances it would have been considered an impossible feat, but the eagerness of the men to get into action with their comrades of the infantry, and the skillful driving, brought them without delay to the very summit, where they went immediately into battle. They were barely in time, for the enemy were also climbing the hill. A close and bloody hand-to-hand struggle ensued, which left both Round Tops in our possession. Weed and Hazlett were killed, and Vincent was mortally wounded—all young men of great promise. . . .

The enemy, however, clung to the woods and rocks at the base of Round Top, carried Devil's Den and its woods, and captured three of Smith's guns, who, however, effectively deprived the enemy of their use by carrying off all the implements.

The breaking in of the Peach Orchard angle exposed the flanks of the batteries on its crests, which retired firing, in order to cover the retreat of the infantry. Many guns of different batteries had to be abandoned because of the destruction of their horses and men; many were hauled off by hand; all the batteries lost heavily. Bigelow's 9th Massachusetts made a stand close by the Trostle house in the corner of the field through which he had retired fighting with prolonges fixed. Although already much cut up, he was directed by McGilvery to hold that point at all hazards until a line of artillery could be formed in front of the wood beyond Plum Run; that is, on what we have called the "Plum Run line." This line was formed by collecting the serviceable batteries, and fragments of batteries, that were brought off, with which, and Dow's Maine battery fresh from the reserve, the pursuit was checked. Finally some 25 guns formed a solid mass, which unsupported by infantry, held this part of the line, aided General Humphreys' movements, and covered by its fire the abandoned guns until they could be brought off, as all were, except perhaps one. When, after accomplishing its purpose, all that was left of Bigelow's battery was withdrawn, it was closely pressed by Colonel Humphreys' 21st Mississippi, the only Confederate regiment which succeeded in crossing the run. His men had entered the battery and fought hand-to-hand with the cannoneers; one was killed whilst trying to spike a gun, and another knocked down with a handspike whilst endeavoring to drag off a prisoner. The battery went into action with 104 officers and men. Of the four battery officers one was killed, another mortally wounded, and a third, Captain Bigelow, severely wounded. Of seven sergeants, two were killed and four wounded; or a total of 28 men, including two missing; and 65 out of 88 horses were killed or wounded. As the battery had sacrificed itself for the safety of the line, its work is specially noticed as typical of the service that artillery is not infrequently called upon to render, and did render in other instances at Gettysburg besides this one.

When Sickles was wounded General Meade directed Hancock to take command of the Third as well as his own corps, which he again turned over to Gibbon. About 7:15 P.M. the field was in a critical condition. Birney's division was now broken up; Humphreys' was slowly falling back, under cover of McGilvery's guns; Anderson's line was advancing. On its right, Barksdale's brigade, except the 21st Mississippi, was held in check only by McGilvery's artillery, to whose support Hancock now brought up Willard's brigade of the Second Corps. Placing the 39th New York in reserve, Willard with his other three regiments charged Barksdale's brigade and drove it back nearly to the Emmitsburg Road, when he was himself repulsed by a heavy artillery and infantry fire, and fell back to his former position near the sources of Plum Run. In this affair Willard was killed and Barksdale mortally wounded. Meanwhile the 21st Mississippi crossed the run from the neighborhood of the Trostle house, and drove out the men of Watson's battery ("I," 5th United States) on the extreme left of McGilvery's line, but was in turn driven

off by the 39th New York, led by Lieutenant Peeples of
the battery, musket in hand, who thus recovered his guns,
Watson being severely wounded.

Birney's division once broken, it was difficult to stem
the tide of defeat. Hood's and McLaws' divisions, excepting Barksdale's brigade, compassed the Devil's Den and
its woods, and as the Federal reenforcements from other
corps came piecemeal, they were beaten in detail until by
successive accretions they greatly outnumbered their oppo-
nents, who had all the advantages of position, when the
latter in turn retired, but were not pursued. This fighting
was confined almost wholly to the woods and wheat field
between the Peach Orchard and Little Round Top, and
the great number of brigade and regimental commanders,
as well as of inferior officers and soldiers, killed and
wounded on both sides, bears testimony to its close and
desperate character. General Meade was on the ground
active in bringing up and putting in reenforcements, and
in doing so had his horse shot under him. At the close
of the day the Confederates held the base of the Round
Tops, Devil's Den, its woods, and the Emmitsburg Road,
with skirmishers thrown out as far as the Trostle house;
the Federals had the two Round Tops, the Plum Run line,
and Cemetery Ridge. During the night the Plum Run
line, except the wood on its left front (occupied by Mc-
Candless's brigade, Crawford's division, his other brigade
being on Big Round Top), was abandoned; the Third
Corps was massed to the left and rear of Caldwell's division, which had reoccupied its short ridge, with McGilvery's artillery on its crest. The Fifth Corps remained on
and about Round Top, and a division (Ruger's) which
had been detached from the Twelfth Corps returned to
Culp's Hill.

When Longstreet's guns were heard, Ewell opened a cannonade, which after an hour's firing was overpowered by the Federal artillery on Cemetery Hill. Johnson's division then advanced, and found only one brigade—Greene's —of the Twelfth Corps in position, the others having been sent to the aid of Sickles at the Peach Orchard. Greene fought with skill and determination for two or three hours, and, reinforced by seven or eight hundred men of the First and Eleventh corps, succeeded in holding his own intrenchments, the enemy taking possession of the abandoned works of Geary and Ruger. This brought Johnson's troops near the Baltimore Pike, but the darkness prevented their seeing or profiting by the advantage then within their reach. When Ruger's division returned from Round Top, and Geary's from Rock Creek, they found Johnson in possession of their intrenchments, and immediately prepared to drive him out at daylight.

It had been ordered that when Johnson engaged Culp's Hill, Early and Rodes should assault Cemetery Hill. Early's attack was made with great spirit, by Hoke's and Avery's brigades, Gordon's being in reserve; the hill was ascended through the wide ravine between Cemetery and Culp's hills, a line of infantry on the slopes was broken, and Wiedrich's Eleventh Corps and Ricketts's reserve batteries near the brow of the hill were overrun; but the excellent position of Stevens's 12-pounders at the head of the ravine, which enabled him to sweep it, the arrival of Carroll's brigade sent unasked by Hancock—a happy inspiration, as this line had been weakened to send supports both to Greene and Sickles—and the failure of Rodes to cooperate with Early, caused the attack to miscarry. The cannoneers of the two batteries, so summarily ousted, rallied and recovered their guns by a vigorous attack—with pistols by those who had them, by others with handspikes, rammers, stones, and even fence-rails—the "Dutchmen" showing that they were in no way inferior to their "Yankee" comrades, who had been taunting them ever since Chancellorsville. After an hour's desperate fighting the enemy was driven out with heavy loss, Avery being among the killed. At the close of this second day a consultation of corps commanders was held at Meade's headquarters. I was not present, although summoned, but was informed that the vote was unanimous to hold our lines and to await an attack for at least one day before taking the offensive, and Meade so decided.

3

The Third Day

A Confederate Report
by Brigadier General
E. Porter Alexander, C.S.A.

Early in the morning General Lee came around, and I was then told that we were to assault Cemetery Hill, which lay rather to our left. This necessitated a good many changes of our positions, which the enemy did not altogether approve of, and they took occasional shots at us, though we shifted about, as inoffensively as possible, and carefully avoided getting into bunches. But we stood it all meekly, and by 10 o'clock, Dearing having come up, we had 75 guns in what was virtually one battery, so disposed as to fire on Cemetery Hill and the batteries south of it, which would have a fire on our advancing infantry. Pickett's division had arrived, and his men were resting and eating. Along Seminary Ridge, a short distance to our left, were 63 guns of A. P. Hill's corps, under Colonel R.

L. Walker. As their distance was a little too great for effective howitzer fire, General Pendleton offered me the use of nine howitzers belonging to that corps. I accepted them, intending to take them into the charge with Pickett; so I put them in a hollow behind a bit of wood, with no orders but to wait there until I sent for them. About 11, some of Hill's skirmishers and the enemy's began fighting over a barn between the lines, and gradually his artillery and the enemy's took part, until over a hundred guns were engaged, and a tremendous roar was kept up for quite a time. But it gradually died out, and the whole field became as silent as a churchyard until 1 o'clock. The enemy, aware of the strength of his position, simply sat still and waited for us. It has been arranged that when the infantry column was ready, General Longstreet should order two guns fired by the Washington Artillery. On that signal all our guns were to open on Cemetery Hill and the ridge extending toward Round Top, which was covered with batteries. I was to observe the fire and give Pickett the order to charge. I accordingly took position, about 12, at the most favorable point, just on the left of the line of guns and with one of Pickett's couriers with me. Soon after I received the following note from Longstreet:

Colonel: If the artillery fire does not have the effect to drive off the enemy or greatly demoralize him, so as to make our efforts pretty certain. I would prefer that you should not advise General Pickett to make the charge. I shall rely a great deal on your good judgment to determine the matter, and shall expect you to let General Pickett know when the moment offers.

This note rather startled me. If that assault was to be made on General Lee's judgment it was all right, but I did

not want it made on mine. I wrote back to General Longstreet to the following effect:

General: I will only be able to judge of the effect of
our fire on the enemy by his return fire, for his infantry
is but little exposed to view and the smoke will obscure
the whole field. If, as I infer from your note, there is
any alternative to this attack, it should be carefully considered before opening our fire, for it will take all the
artillery ammunition we have left to test this one thoroughly, and, if the result is unfavorable, we will have
none left for another effort. And even if this is entirely
successful, it can only be so at a very bloody cost.

To this presently came the following reply:

Colonel: The intention is to advance the infantry if
the artillery has the desired effect of driving the enemy's
off, or having other effect such as to warrant us in making the attack. When the moment arrives advise General
Pickett, and of course advance such artillery as you can
use in aiding the attack.

I hardly knew whether this left me discretion or not,
but at any rate it seemed decided that the artillery must
open. I felt that if we went that far we could not draw
back, but the infantry must go too. General A. R. Wright,
of Hill's corps, was with me looking at the position when
these notes were received, and we discussed them together.
Wright said, "It is not so hard to *go* there as it looks; I
was nearly there with my brigade yesterday. The trouble
is to *stay* there. The whole Yankee army is there in a
bunch."

I was influenced by this, and somewhat by a sort of
camp rumor which I had heard that morning, that General Lee had said that he was going to send every man he

had upon that hill. At any rate, I assumed that the question of supports had been well considered, and that whatever was possible would be done. But before replying I rode to see Pickett, who was with his division a short distance in the rear. I did not tell him my object, but only tried to guess how he felt about the charge. He seemed very sanguine, and thought himself in luck to have the chance. Then I felt that I could not make any delay or let the attack suffer by any indecision on my part. And, that General Longstreet might know of my intention, I wrote him only this: "General: When our artillery fire is at its best, I shall order Pickett to charge."

Then, getting a little more anxious, I decided to send for the nine howitzers and take them ahead of Pickett up nearly to musket range, instead of following close behind him as at first intended; so I sent a courier to bring them up in front of the infantry, but under cover of the wood. The courier could not find them. He was sent again, and only returned after our fire was opened, saying they were gone. I afterward learned that General Pendleton had sent for a part of them, and the others had moved to a neighboring hollow to get out of the line of the enemy's fire at one of Hill's batteries during the artillery duel they had had an hour before.

At exactly 1 o'clock by my watch the two signal guns were heard in quick succession. In another minute every gun was at work. The enemy were not slow in coming back at us, and the grand roar of nearly the whole artillery of both armies burst in on the silence, almost as suddenly as the full notes of an organ would fill a church.

The artillery of Ewell's corps, however, took only a small part, I believe, in this, as they were too far away on the other side of the town. Some of them might have done good service from positions between Hill and Ewell, enfilading the batteries fighting us. The opportunity to do that was the single advantage in our having the exterior line, to compensate for all its disadvantages. But our line was so extended that all of it was not well studied, and the officers of the different corps had no opportunity to examine each other's ground for chances to cooperate.

The enemy's position seemed to have broken out with guns everywhere, and from Round Top to Cemetery Hill was blazing like a volcano. The air seemed full of missiles from every direction. . . .

Before the cannonade opened I had made up my mind to give Pickett the order to advance within fifteen or twenty minutes after it began. But when I looked at the full development of the enemy's batteries, and knew that his infantry was generally protected from our fire by stone walls and swells of the ground, I could not bring myself to give the word. It seemed madness to launch infantry into that fire, with nearly three-quarters of a mile to go at midday under a July sun. I let the 15 minutes pass, and 20, and 25, hoping vainly for something to turn up. Then I wrote to Pickett: "If you are coming at all you must come at once, or I cannot give you proper support; but the enemy's fire has not slackened at all; at least 18 guns are still firing from the cemetery itself." Five minutes after sending that message, the enemy's fire suddenly began to slacken, and the guns in the cemetery limbered up and vacated the position.

We Confederates often did such things as that to save our ammunition for use against infantry, but I had never before seen the Federals withdraw their guns simply to save them up for the infantry fight. So I said, "If he does not run fresh batteries in there in five minutes, this is our fight." I looked anxiously with my glass, and the five minutes passed without a sign of life on the deserted position, still swept by our fire, and littered with dead men and horses and fragments of disabled carriages. Then I wrote Pickett, urgently: "For God's sake, come quick. The eighteen guns are gone; come quick, or my ammunition won't let me support you properly."

I afterward heard from others what took place with my first note to Pickett.

Pickett took it to Longstreet; Longstreet read it, and said nothing. Pickett said, "General, shall I advance?" Longstreet, knowing it had to be, but unwilling to give the word, turned his face away. Pickett saluted and said, "I am going to move forward, sir," galloped off to his division and immediately put it in motion.

Longstreet, leaving his staff, came out alone to where I was. It was then about 1:40 P.M. I explained the situation, feeling then more hopeful, but afraid our artillery ammunition might not hold out for all we would want. Longstreet said, "Stop Pickett immediately and replenish your ammunition." I explained that it would take too long, and the enemy would recover from the effect our fire was then having, and we had, moreover, very little to replenish with. Longstreet said, "I don't want to make this attack. I would stop it now but that General Lee ordered it and expects it to go on. I don't see how it can succeed."

I listened, but did not dare offer a word. The battle was lost if we stopped. Ammunition was far too low to try anything else, for we had been fighting three days. There was a chance, and it was not my part to interfere. While Longstreet was still speaking, Pickett's division swept out of the wood and showed the full length of its gray ranks and shining bayonets, as grand a sight as ever a man looked on. Joining it on the left, Pettigrew stretched farther than I could see. General Dick Garnett, just out of the sick ambulance, and buttoned up in an old blue overcoat, riding at the head of his brigade passed us and saluted Longstreet. Garnett was a warm personal friend, and we had not met before for months. We had served on the plains together before the war. I rode with him a short distance, and then we wished each other luck and a good-bye, which was our last.

Then I rode down the line of guns, selecting such as had enough ammunition to follow Pickett's advance, and starting them after him as fast as possible. I got, I think, 15 or 18 in all, in a little while, and went with them. Meanwhile, the infantry had no sooner debouched on the plain than all the enemy's line, which had been nearly silent, broke out again with all its batteries. The 18 guns were back in the cemetery, and a storm of shell began bursting over and among our infantry. All of our guns, silent as the infantry passed between them, reopened over their heads when the lines had got a couple of hundred yards away, but the enemy's artillery let us alone and fired only at the infantry. No one could have looked at that advance without feeling proud of it.

But, as our supporting guns advanced, we passed many poor, mangled victims left in its trampled wake. A terrific infantry fire was now opened upon Pickett, and a considerable force of the enemy moved out to attack the right flank of his line. We halted, unlimbered, and opened fire upon it. Pickett's men never halted, but opened fire at close range, swarmed over the fences and among the enemy's guns, were swallowed up in smoke, and that was the last of them. The conflict hardly seemed to last five minutes before they were melted away, and only disorganized stragglers pursued by a moderate fire were coming back. Just then, Wilcox's brigade passed by us, moving to Pickett's support. There was no longer anything to support, and with the keenest pity at the useless waste of life, I saw them advance. The men, as they passed us, looked bewildered, as if they wondered what they were expected to do, or why they were there. However, they were soon halted and moved back. They suffered some losses, and we had a few casualties from canister sent at them at rather long range.

From the position of our guns the sight of this conflict was grand and thrilling, and we watched it as men with a life-and-death interest in the result. If it should be favorable to us, the war was nearly over; if against us, we each had the risks of many battles yet to go through. And the event culminated with fearful rapidity. Listening to the rolling crashes of musketry, it was hard to realize that they were made up of single reports, and that each musketshot represented nearly a minute of a man's life in that storm of lead and iron. It seemed as if 100,000 men were engaged, and that human life was being poured out like water. As soon as it appeared that the assault had failed, we ceased firing in order to save ammunition in case the enemy should advance. But we held our ground as boldly as possible, though we were entirely without support, and very low in ammunition. The enemy gave us an occasional shot for a while and then, to our great relief, let us rest. About that time General Lee, entirely alone, rode up and remained with me for a long time. He then probably first appreciated the full extent of the disaster as the disorganized stragglers made their way back past us. The Comte de Paris, in his excellent account of this battle, remarks that Lee, as a soldier, must at this moment have foreseen Appomattox—that he must have realized that he could never again muster so powerful an army, and that for the future he could only delay, but not avert, the failure of his cause. However this may be, it was certainly a momentous thing to him to see that superb attack end in such a bloody repulse. But, whatever his emotions, there was no trace of them in his calm and self-possessed bearing. I thought at the time his coming there very imprudent, and the absence of all his staff officers and couriers strange. It could only have happened by his express intention. I have since thought it possible that he came, thinking the enemy might follow in pursuit of Pickett, personally to rally stragglers about our guns and make a desperate defense. He had the instincts of a soldier within him as strongly as any man. Looking at Burnside's dense columns swarming through the fire of our guns toward Marye's Hill at Fredericksburg, he had said: "It is well war is so terrible or we would grow too fond of it." No soldier could have looked on at Pickett's charge and not burned to be in it. To have a personal part in a close and desperate fight at that moment would, I believe, have been at heart a great pleasure to General Lee, and possibly he was looking for one. We were here joined by Colonel Fremantle of Her Majesty's Coldstream Guards, who was visiting our army. He afterward published an excellent account of the battle in "Blackwood," and described many little incidents that took place here, such as General Lee's encouraigng the retreating stragglers to rally as soon as they got back to cover, and saying that the failure was his fault, not theirs. Colonel Fremantle especially noticed that General Lee reproved an officer for spurring a foolish horse, and advised him to use only gentle measures. The officer was Lieutenant F. M. Colston of my staff, whom General Lee had requested to ride off to the right and try to discover the cause of a great cheering we heard in the enemy's lines. We thought it might mean an advance upon us, but it proved to be only a greeting to some general officer riding along the line.

That was the end of the battle. . . . Night came very slowly, but came at last; and about 10 the last gun was withdrawn to Willoughby Run, whence we had moved to the attack the afternoon before.

Of Pickett's three brigadiers, Garnett and Armistead were killed and Kemper dangerously wounded. Fry, who commanded Pettigrew's brigade, which adjoined Garnett on the left, and in the charge was the brigade of direction for the whole force, was also left on the field desperately wounded. Of all Pickett's field officers in the three brigades only one major came out unhurt. The men who made the attack were good enough: the only trouble was, there were not enough of them.

Pickett's Messages

Before advancing on the Federal center, Pickett handed Longstreet a letter to be mailed to a girl in Richmond to whom he was engaged to marry. Penciled on the back of the envelope were the words:: "If Old Peter's (Longstreet's) nod means death, good-by, and God bless you, little one."

He came out of it alive and wrote to his Virginia girl: "Your soldier lives and mourns and but for you, he would rather, a million times rather, be back here with his dead to sleep for all time in an unknown grave."

A Union Report
by Major General Henry J. Hunt, U.S.A.

In view of the successes gained on the second day, General Lee resolved to renew his efforts. These successes were:

On the right, the lodgment at the bases of the Round Tops, the possession of Devil's Den and its woods, and the ridges on the Emmitsburg Road, which gave him the coveted positions for his artillery.

On the left, the occupation of part of the intrenchments of the Twelfth Corps, with an outlet to the Baltimore Pike, by which all our lines could be taken in reverse.

At the center, the partial success of three of Anderson's brigades in penetrating our lines, from which they were expelled only because they lacked proper support. It was thought that better concert of action might have made good a lodgment here also.

Both armies had indeed lost heavily, but the account in that respect seemed in favor of the Confederates, or at worst, balanced. Pickett's and Edward Johnson's divisions were fresh, as were Posey's and Mahone's brigades of R. H. Anderson's, and William Smith's brigade of Early's division. These could be depended upon for an assault; the others could be used as supports, and to follow up a success. The artillery was almost intact. Stuart had arrived with his cavalry, excepting the brigades of Jones and Robertson, guarding the communications; and Imboden had also come up. General Lee, therefore, directed the renewal of operations both on the right and left. Ewell had been ordered to attack at daylight on July 3rd, and during the night reenforced Johnson with Smith's, Dan-

iel's, and O'Neal's brigades. Johnson had made his preparations, and was about moving, when at dawn William's
artillery opened upon him, preparatory to an assault by
Geary and Ruger for the recovery of their works. The sus-
pension of this fire was followed by an immediate advance
by both sides. A conflict ensued which lasted with varying
success until nearly 11 o'clock, during which the Confederates were driven out of the Union intrenchments by Geary
and Ruger, aided by Shaler's brigade of the Sixth Corps.
They made one or two attempts to regain possession, but
were unsuccessful, and a demonstration to turn Johnson's
left caused him to withdraw his command to Rock Creek.
At the close of the war the scene of this conflict was covered by a forest of dead trees, leaden bullets proving as
fatal to them as to the soldiers whose bodies were thickly
strewn beneath them.

Longstreet's arrangements had been made to attack
Round Top, and his orders issued with a view to turning
it, when General Lee decided that the assault should be
made on Cemetery Ridge by Pickett's and Pettigrew's divisions, with part of Trimble's. Longstreet formed these in
two lines—Pickett on the right, supported by Wilcox; Pettigrew on the left, with Lane's and Scales's brigades under
Trimble in the second line. Hill was ordered to hold his
line with the remainder of his corps, six brigades, give
Longstreet assistance if required, and avail himself of any
success that might be gained. Finally a powerful artillery
force, about 150 guns, was ordered to prepare the way for
the assault by cannonade. The necessary arrangements
caused delay, and before notice of this could be received
by Ewell, Johnson, as we have seen, was attacked, so that
the contest was over on the left before that at the center

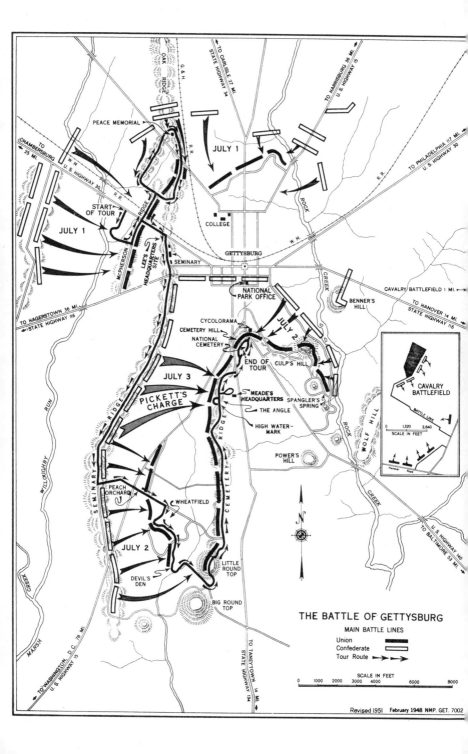

THE BATTLE OF GETTYSBURG

MAIN BATTLE LINES

Union
Confederate
Tour Route

SCALE IN FEET
0   1000   2000   3000   4000   6000   8000

Revised 1951   February 1948 NMP. GET. 7002

SERGEANT . . . 1ST UNITED STATES CAVALRY

This sergeant is one of the hard-bitten regulars, and wears the short 12-button cavalry jacket, dark blue, trimmed with yellow piping. Chevrons are yellow, the color of the cavalry arm. The carbine, slung over his left shoulder by the three-inch sling, is a Spencer repeating arm, holding seven .50 cal. rf cartridges, loaded into a magazine tube in the butt. On his right hip, with butt forward, is a Colt's 1860 Army model revolver, cal. .44. His saber is the Chickopee light cavalry model with leather saber knot. The knee-cap heavy boots were standard issue. His trousers are sky-blue, with a 1½-inch yellow stripe along the seams . . . regulation for his rank. His forage cap carries the brass crossed sabers of the cavalry arm.

COPYRIGHT 1964 DONALD F. DOW

BERDAN'S SHARPSHOOTER . . . MORRELL'S DIVISION

Uniformed and equipped the same as other infantrymen, this Union sharpshooter does have a different type rifle. While many of Berdan's Sharpshooters were equipped with the Sharps .52 cal. rifles, a few experts in long range shooting equipped themselves with privately made telescopic-sight rifles. This one is a rifled .44 cal., with a heavy 33-inch barrel, made by George W. Leonard, Keene, N. H. With its adjustable double set triggers, and 37½ inch telescope sight it enabled the corporal carrying it to be a deadly threat to Confederate safety.

PRIVATE . . . TENNESSEE INFANTRY

This soldier is clothed and equipped in a manner that exemplifies the South's lack of uniform military equipment. His C. S. belt buckle may be the only regulation piece of equipment he has . . . but he does have the essentials for making himself useful in battle . . . no matter where these essentials came from. His rifle is the English imported Enfield, caliber .577, equipped with a triangular bayonet. On his belt is a cap pouch, a heavy knife, and around to the back, a bullet pouch. The blanket rolled and tied around a shoulder, cup and canteen complete his meager equipment. The trouser legs are wrapped at the bottoms with strips of cloth, serving as short leggings. His clothes are whatever he could get . . . hickory shirt, old felt hat . . . and those shoes . . . no doubt Yankee!

When McLaw's Confederate Division broke through the salient at the Peach Orchard on the afternoon of the second day, it was met at Plum Run by a charge of the Pennsylvania Reserves, some of whom fought within sight of their own homes. Painted in 1881 by Peter Fredrick Rothermel. (Courtesy of Pennsylvania State Museum)

From 4 in the morning until 11 A.M. of July 3, 1863, the third
and last day of the Battle of Gettysburg, fighting raged for the
possession of the breastworks on Culp's Hill. Artist Rothermel's conception of the repulse of Major General Edward
Johnson's Confederate Division by Brigadier General John W.
Geary's White Star Division. (Courtesy of Pennsylvania State
Museum)

Charge of the Louisiana Tigers and repulse on East Cemetery Hill in the evening of July 2. Painted by Peter Frederick Rothermel. (Courtesy of Pennsylvania State Museum)

PIKEMAN . . . 5TH GEORGIA INFANTRY

Not having enough firearms to arm all Confederate troops, some ancient type weapons were issued to some units in desperation. In July of 1862 Governor Joseph E. Brown of Georgia called on the mechanics of his state to furnish the state military units with "Georgia Pikes" . . . according to his specifications to be on "a six-foot staff with the side knife, eighteen-inch blade, weighing about three pounds." The Georgia Pike shown here is a variation of the model called for, being a clover-leaf bridle-cutting pike, with 10″ blade and 3¼″ side blades. About 2500 of these weapons were made and turned into the arsenal and later given out to Georgia soldiers to repel Sherman's army. The pikeman is wearing a gray forage cap with the number of his regiment, a Confederate lion's head buckle imported from England, a .31 cal. captured Colt's revolver, pocket model of 1849, and an Ames artillery sword, model of 1832.

UNINTENDED ACCURACY—BULLETS THAT MET IN MIDAIR

Top: Confederate Enfield on left, caliber .577, and Springfield rifle bullet on right, caliber .58. Note wooden plug still retained in Enfield bullet.

Bottom: A most unusual circumstance occasioned the joining of these bullets. Both Confederates, a faster velocity Enfield bullet overtook a slower moving .69 caliber bullet. (From Battlefield of Resaca, Georgia, 1864)

CORPORAL . . . WHEELER'S CAVALRY

Except for his grey shirt and trousers, this Confederate trooper is equipped with captured Union gear. His carbine is a Sharps breechloader; the saber at his side is a Chickopee, standard issue of the Federal mounted service, and the pistol on his hip is a Colt's 1860 army model percussion revolver. Belt buckle is a brass C. S. one, cast in the South, and his light colored felt hat is adorned with the typical yellow ostrich plume of the Confederate cavalry. On his feet are a pair of boots taken from a Yankee cavalry man . . . complete with northern-made brass spurs.

PRIVATE . . . 81ST OHIO VOLUNTEERS

The equipment shown on this volunteer infantryman was
standard issue to both regular and volunteer units the last
two years of the war. His rifle is the Model 1860 Springfield
muzzle-loader, caliber .58, equipped with angular bayonet.
The knapsack on his back contains rations, gun cleaning kit,
extra shoes and socks . . . topped by a tightly rolled blanket.
On his left hip are suspended a spacious canvas haversack and
a metal canteen. A huge cartridge box rests on his right hip
. . . suspended from the shoulder by a broad leather strap.
On his oval U. S. buckled belt is his cap pouch. The blue forage cap has the standard infantry insignia pinned to the front
. . . a curved horn. The dark blue blouse is his field dress;
trousers are sky-blue, and are enclosed at the bottom by canvas
leggings.

COLONEL . . . CONFEDERATE CAVALRY

Uniform variety in the Confederate army was great, but this officer's short cavalry jacket, trimmed with yellow collar and cuff facings, and with gold braid galons on the sleeves denoting rank according to the number of rows of braid. Confederate officers wore no shoulder tabs . . . rank insignia, besides sleeve galons, was indicated by the stiff standing collars. This Colonel is armed with a percussion revolver, probably a captured Colt army or navy model, and a saber . . . either captured from the Yankees or imported from England or France. His belt buckle is a brass officer's type, with the letters C. S. Boots and spurs are one of many varieties used by both sides. The hat is a common style, of soft felt, turned up on the right, with a yellow ostrich plume on the left.

LT. COL. . . . 6TH N. Y. VOLUNTEER CAVALRY

Dressed strictly according to regulation, except for the unbuttoned coat, this Union cavalry officer bears the percussion revolver and saber with which the cavalry was armed. The Colt 1860 Army model is .44 caliber; caps for this arm are carried in the oval leather pouch fastened to the belt, and paper-wrapped cartridges would probably be found in a leather box attached to the back of the belt. The belt plate is the standard one found on all sword belts . . . a little more highly ornamented on officers than the straight brass enlisted man's model . . . but the same patterns. The sash is yellow silk net, with silk bullion fringes. His saber is the standard Chickopee cavalry saber, equipped with a sturdy leather sword knot. This Lt. Colonel's shoulder strap is cloth, with embroidered trim and rank device . . . silver oak leaves in this case. Boots are regulation knee cap style, with brass roweled spurs. His cap is the Union forage cap, and his dark blue coat has black velvet collar and cuffs.

Best Regards to
Ed Ammann from
the ol' Rebel Jimi White
1954

FORREST'S CAVALRY,
CONFEDERATE STATES
ARMY

F. BEARDWEE
'54

The first safe-functioning repeating rifle, the Spencer, was well balanced and accurate. Seven .50 caliber, revolutionary, brass, rimfire cartridges filled a tube which was inserted in the butt of the stock, and an eighth could be placed in the chamber. With this, a new dimension in firepower was first put into operation by dismounted Federal cavalrymen the last week of June, 1863. (Courtesy of Smithsonian Institution)

was begun. The hoped-for concert of action in the Confederate attacks was lost from the beginning.

On the Federal side Hancock's corps held Cemetery Ridge with Robinson's division, First Corps, on Hay's right in support, and Doubleday's at the angle between Gibbon and Caldwell. General Newton, having been assigned to the command of the First Corps, *vice* Reynolds, was now in charge of the ridge held by Caldwell. Compactly arranged on its crest was McGilvery's artillery, 41 guns, consisting of his own batteries, reenforced by others from the Artillery Reserve. Well to the right, in front of Hays and Gibbon, was the artillery of the Second Corps under its chief, Captain Hazard. Woodruff's battery was in front of Ziegler's Grove; on his left, in succession, Arnold's Rhode Island, Cushing's United States, Brown's Rhode Island, and Rorty's New York. In the fight of the preceding day the two last-named batteries had been to the front and suffered severely. Lieutenant T. Fred Brown was severely wounded, and his command devolved on Lieutenant Perrin. So great had been the loss in men and horses that they were now of four guns each, reducing the total number in the corps to 26. Daniel's battery of horse artillery, four guns, was at the angle. Cowan's 1st New York battery, six rifles, was placed on the left of Rorty's soon after the cannonade commenced. In addition, some of the guns on Cemetery Hill, and Rittenhouse's on Little Round Top, could be brought to bear, but these were offset by batteries similarly placed on the flanks of the enemy, so that on the Second Corps line, within the space of a mile, were 77 guns to oppose nearly 150. They were on an open crest plainly visible from all parts of the opposite line. Between 10 and 11 A.M., everything looking favorable at

Culp's Hill, I crossed over to Cemetery Ridge, to see what might be going on at other points. Here a magnificent display greeted my eyes. Our whole front for two miles was covered by batteries already in line or going into position. They stretched—apparently in one unbroken mass —from opposite the town to the Peach Orchard, which bounded the view to the left, the ridges of which were planted thick with cannon. Never before had such a sight been witnessed on this continent, and rarely, if ever, abroad. What did it mean? It might possibly be to hold that line while its infantry was sent to aid Ewell, or to guard against a counterstroke from us, but it most probably meant an assault on our center, to be preceded by a cannonade in order to crush our batteries and shake our infantry; at least to cause us to exhaust our ammunition in reply, so that the assaulting troops might pass in good condition over the half mile of open ground which was beyond our effective musketry fire. With such an object the cannonade would be long and followed immediately by the assault, their whole army being held in readiness to follow up a success. From the great extent of ground occupied by the enemy's batteries, it was evident that all the artillery on our west front, whether of the army corps or the reserve, must concur as a *unit,* under the chief of artillery, in the defense. This is provided for in all well-organized armies by special rules, which formerly were contained in our own army regulations, but they had been condensed in successive editions into a few short lines, so obscure as to be virtually worthless, because, like the rudimentary toe of the dog's paw, they had become, from lack of use, mere survivals—unintelligible except to the specialist. It was of the first importance to subject the enemy's infantry, from the first moment of their advance, to such a cross fire of our artillery as would break their formation, check their impulse, and drive them back, or at least bring them to our lines in such condition as to make them an easy prey. There was neither time nor necessity for reporting this to General Meade, and beginning on the right, I instructed the chiefs of artillery and battery commanders to withhold their fire for 15 or 20 minutes after the cannonade commenced, then to concentrate their fire with all possible accuracy on those batteries which were most destructive to us, but slowly, so that when the enemy's ammunition was exhausted, we should have sufficient left to meet the assault. I had just given these orders to the last battery on Little Round Top, when the signal gun was fired, and the enemy opened with all his guns. From that point the scene was indescribably grand. All their batteries were soon covered with smoke, through which the flashes were incessant, whilst the air seemed filled with shells, whose sharp explosions, with the hurtling of their fragments, formed a running accompaniment to the deep roar of the guns. Thence I rode to the Artillery Reserve to order fresh batteries and ammunition to be sent up to the ridge as soon as the cannonade ceased; but both the reserve and the train had gone to a safer place. Messengers, however, had been left to receive and convey orders, which I sent by them; then I returned to the ridge. Turning into the Taneytown Pike, I saw evidence of the necessity under which the reserve had "decamped," in the remains of a dozen exploded caissons, which had been placed under cover of a hill, but which the shells had managed to search out. In fact, the fire was more dangerous behind the ridge than on its crest, which I soon reached at the position occupied by General Newton behind McGilvery's batteries, from which we had a fine view as all our own guns were now in action.

Most of the enemy's projectiles passed overhead, the effect being to sweep all the open ground in our rear, which was of little benefit to the Confederates—a mere waste of ammunition, for everything here could seek shelter. And just here an incident already published may be repeated, as it illustrates a peculiar feature of civil war. Colonel Long, who was at the time on General Lee's staff, had a few years before served in my mounted battery expressly to receive a course of instruction in the use of field artillery. At Appomattox we spent several hours together, and in the course of conversation I told him I was not satisfied with the conduct of this cannonade which I had heard was under his direction, inasmuch as he had not done justice to his instruction; that his fire, instead of being concentrated on the point of attack, as it ought to have been, and as I expected it would be, was scattered over the whole field. He was amused at the criticism and said: "I remembered my lessons at the time, and when the fire became so scattered, wondered what you would think about it!"

The Confederate approach was magnificent, and excited our admiration; but the story of that charge is so well known that I need not dwell upon it further than as it concerns my own command. The steady fire from McGilvery and Rittenhouse, on their right, caused Pickett's men to "drift" in the opposite direction, so that the weight of the assault fell upon the positions occupied by Hazard's batteries. I had counted on an artillery cross fire that would stop it before it reached our lines, but, except a few shots here and there, Hazard's batteries were silent until the enemy came within canister range. They had unfortunately exhausted their long range projectiles during the cannonade, under the orders of their corps commander, and it was too late to replace them. Had my instructions been followed here, as they were by McGilvery, I do not believe that Pickett's division would have reached our line. We lost not only the fire of one-third of our guns, but the resulting cross fire, which would have doubled its value. The prime fault was in the obscurity of our army regulations as to the artillery, and the absence of all regulations as to the proper relations of the different arms of service to one another. On this occasion it cost us much blood, many lives, and for a moment endangered the integrity of our line if not the success of the battle. Soon after Pickett's repulse, Wilcox's, Wright's, and Perry's brigades were moved forward, but under the fire of the fresh batteries in Gibbon's front, of McGilvery's and Rittenhouse's guns and the advance of two regiments of Stannard's Vermont brigade, they soon fell back. The losses in the batteries of the Second Corps were very heavy. Of the five battery commanders and their successors on the field, Rorty, Cushing, and Woodruff were killed, and Milne was mortally and Sheldon severely wounded at their guns. So great was the destruction of men and horses, that Cushing's and Woodruff's United States, and Brown's and Arnold's Rhode Island batteries were consolidated to form two serviceable ones.

The advance of the Confederate brigades to cover Pickett's retreat showed that the enemy's line opposite Cemetery Ridge was occupied by infantry. Our own line on the ridge was in more or less disorder, as the result of the conflict, and in no condition to advance a sufficient force for a counterassault. The largest bodies of organized troops available were on the left, and General Meade now proceeded to Round Top and pushed out skirmishers to feel the enemy in its front. An advance to the Plum Run line, of the troops behind it, would have brought them directly in front of the numerous batteries which crowned the Emmitsburg Ridge, commanding that line and all the intervening ground; a farther advance, to the attack, would have brought them under additional heavy flank fires. McCandless's brigade, supported by Nevin's, was, however, pushed forward, under cover of the woods, which protected them from the fire of all these batteries; it crossed the Wheatfield, cleared the woods, and had an encounter with a portion of Benning's brigade, which was retiring. Hood's and McLaws's divisions were falling back under Longstreet's orders to their strong position, resting on Peach Orchard and covering Hill's line. Our troops on the left were locked up. As to the center, Pickett's and Pettigrew's assaulting divisions had formed no part of A. P. Hill's line, which was virtually intact. The idea that there must have been "a gap of at least a mile" in that line, made by throwing forward these divisions, and that a prompt advance from Cemetery Ridge would have given us the line, or the artillery in front of it, was a delusion. A prompt countercharge after a combat between two small bodies of men is one thing; the change from the defensive to the offensive of an army, after an engagement at a single *point,* is quite another. *This* was not a "Waterloo defeat" with a fresh army to follow it up, and to have made such a change to the offensive, on the assumption that Lee had made no provision against a reverse, would have been rash in the extreme. An advance of 20,000 men from Cemetery Ridge in the face of the 140 guns then in position would have been stark madness; an immediate advance from any point, in force, was simply impracticable, and before due preparation could have been made for a change to the offensive, the favorable moment—had any resulted from the repulse—would have passed away.

Whilst the main battle was raging, sharp cavalry combats took place on both flanks of the army. On the left the principal incident was an attack made by order of General Kilpatrick on infantry and artillery in woods and behind stone fences, which resulted in considerable losses, and especially in the death of General Farnsworth, a gallant and promising officer who had but a few days before been appointed brigadier general and had not yet received his commission. On the right an affair of some magnitude took place between Stuart's command of four and Gregg's of three brigades; but Jenkins's Confederate brigade was soon thrown out of action from lack of ammunition, and two only of Gregg's were engaged. Stuart had been ordered to cover Ewell's left and was proceeding toward the Baltimore Pike, where he hoped to create a diversion in aid of the Confederate infantry, and in case of Pickett's success to fall upon the retreating Federal troops. From near Cress's Ridge, two and a half miles east of Gettysburg, Stuart commanded a view of the roads in rear of the Federal lines. On its northern wooded end he posted Jackson's battery, and took possession of the Rummel farm buildings, a few hundred yards distant. Hampton and Fitzhugh Lee were on his left, covered by the wood, Jenkins and Chambliss on the right, along the ridge. Half a mile east on a low parallel ridge, the southern part of which bending west toward Cress's Ridge furnished excellent positions for artillery, was the Federal cavalry brigade of McIntosh, who now sent a force toward Rummel's, from which a strong body of skirmishers was thrown to meet them, and the battery opened. McIntosh now demanded reenforcements, and Gregg, then near the Baltimore Pike, brought him Custer's brigade and Pennington's and Randol's batteries. The artillery soon drove the Confederates out of Rummel's, and compelled Jackson's Virginia battery to leave the ridge. Both sides brought up reenforcements and the battle swayed from side to side of the interval. Finally the Federals were pressed back, and Lee and Hampton, emerging from the wood, charged, sword in hand, facing a destructive artillery fire—for the falling back of the cavalry had uncovered our batteries. The assailants were met by Custer's and such other mounted squadrons as could be thrown in; a melee ensued, in which Hampton was severely wounded and the charge repulsed. Breathed's and McGregor's Confederate batteries had replaced Jackson's, a sharp artillery duel took place, and at nightfall each side held substantially its original ground. Both sides claim to have held the Rummel house. The advantage was deceidedly with the Federals, who had foiled Stuart's plans. Thus the battle of Gettysburg closed as it had opened, with a very creditable cavalry battle.

General Lee now abandoned the attempt to dislodge Meade, intrenched a line from Oak Hill to Peach Orchard, started all his *impedimenta* to the Potomac in advance, and followed with his army on the night of July 4th, via Fairfield. . . .

But the hopes and expectations excited by the victory of Gettysburg were as unreasonable as the fears that had preceded it; and great was the disappointment that followed the "escape" of Lee's army. It was promptly manifested, too, and in a manner which indicates how harshly and unjustly the Army of the Potomac and its commanders were usually judged and treated; and what trials the latter had to undergo whilst subjected to the meddling and hectoring of a distant superior, from which they were not freed until the general-in-chief accompanied them in the field. On the day following Lee's withdrawal, before it was possible that all the circumstances could be known, three dispatches passed between the respective headquarters:

Halleck to Meade July 14 (*in part*) : "I need hardly say to you that the escape of Lee's army without another battle has created great dissatisfaction in the mind of the President, and it will require an active and energetic pursuit on your part to remove the impression that it has not been sufficiently active heretofore."

Meade to Halleck July 14: "Having performed my duty conscientiously and to the best of my ability, the censure of the President conveyed in your dispatch of 1 P.M. this day, is in my judgment, so undeserved that I feel compelled most respectfully to ask to be immediately relieved from the command of this army."

Halleck to Meade July 14th: "My telegram stating the disappointment of the President at the escape of Lee's army was not intended as a censure, but as a stimulus to an active pursuit. It is not deemed a sufficient cause of your application to be relieved."

Whatever the object of these dispatches of General Halleck, they are perfectly consistent with a determination on the part of the War Department to discredit under all circumstances the Army of the Potomac and any commander identified with it—and that was the effect in this case.

4

Diary of the Three-Day Battle

by Lieutenant Colonel Arthur J. L. Fremantle

A guest of General Lee during the Gettysburg campaign, Colonel Fremantle, after his return to his home in England, included in his book, *Three Months in the Southern States,* his diary account of July 1, 2 and 3, 1863.

July 1st (Wednesday). At 4:30 P.M. we came in sight of Gettysburg, and joined General Lee and General Hill, who were on the top of one of the ridges which form a peculiar feature of the country round Gettysburg. We could see the enemy retreating up one of the opposite ridges, pursued by the Confederates with loud yells. The position into which the enemy had been driven was evidently a strong one. His right appeared to rest on a cemetery, on the top of a high ridge to the right of Gettysburg, as we looked at it.

General Hill now came up and told me he had been

very unwell all day, and in fact he looks very delicate. He said he had two divisions engaged, and had driven the enemy four miles into the present position, capturing a great many prisoners, some cannon, and some colors. He said, however, that the Yankees had fought with a determination unusual to them.

July 2nd (Thursday). At 2 P.M. General Longstreet advised me, if I wished to have a good view of the battle, to return to my tree of yesterday. I did so and remained there with Lawly and Captain Schreibert during the rest of the afternoon. But until 4:45 P.M. all was profoundly quiet, and we began to doubt whether a fight was coming off today at all. At that time, however, Longstreet suddenly commenced a heavy cannonade on the right. Ewell immediately took it up on the left. The enemy replied with equal fury, and in a few moments the firing along the whole line was as heavy as it is possible to conceive. A dense smoke arose for six miles; there was little wind to drive it away, and the air seemed full of shells, each of which appeared to have a different style of going, and made a different noise from the others. The ordnance on both sides is of a very varied description. Every now and then a caisson would blow up—if a Federal one, a Confederate yell would immediately follow. The Southern troops, when charging, or to express their delight, always yell in a manner peculiar to themselves. The Yankee cheer is much like ours, but the Confederate officers declare that the Rebel yell has a particular merit, and always produces a salutary effect upon their adversaries. A corps is sometimes spoken of as "a good yelling regiment."

As soon as the firing began, General Lee joined Hill just below our tree, and he remained there nearly all the time, looking through his field glasses, sometimes talking to Hill and sometimes to Colonel Long of his staff. But generally he sat quite alone on the stump of a tree. What I remarked especially was, that during the whole time the firing continued, he sent only one message, and received only one report. It evidently is his system to arrange the plan thoroughly with the three commanders, and then leave them the duty of modifying and carrying it out to the best of their abilities.

When the cannonade was at its height, a Confederate band of music, between the cemetery and ourselves, began to play polkas and waltzes, which sounded very curious, accompanied by the hissing and bursting of the shells.

At 5:45 all became comparatively quiet on our left and in the cemetery; but volleys of musketry on the right told us that Longstreet's infantry were advancing, and the onward progress of the smoke showed that he was progressing favorably; but about 6:30 there seemed to be a check, and even a slight retrograde movement.

. . . A little before dark the firing dropped off in every direction, and soon ceased altogether. We then received intelligence that Longstreet had carried everything before him for some time, capturing several batteries and driving the enemy from his positions; but when Hill's Florida brigade and some other troops gave way, he was forced to abandon a small portion of the ground he had won, together with all the captured guns except three. His troops, however, bivouacked during the night on ground occupied by the enemy in the morning.

July 3rd (Friday). At 2:30 P.M., after passing General Lee and his staff, I rode on through the woods in the direction in which I had left Longstreet. I soon began to meet many wounded men returning from the front; many of them asked in piteous tones the way to a doctor or an ambulance. The further I got, the greater became the number of wounded. At last I came to a perfect stream of them flocking through the woods in numbers as great as the crowd in Oxford Street in the middle of the day. Some were walking alone on crutches composed of two rifles, others were supported by men less badly wounded than themselves, and others carried on stretchers by the ambulance corps, but in no case did I see a sound man helping the wounded to the rear unless he carried the red badge of the ambulance corps. They were still under heavy fire, the shells bringing down great limbs of trees, and carrying further destruction amongst this melancholy procession. I saw all this in much less time than it takes to write it, and although astonished to meet such vast numbers of wounded, I had not seen enough to give me any idea of the real extent of the mischief.

When I got close up to General Longstreet, I saw one of his regiments advancing through the woods in good order; so, thinking I was just in time to see the attack, I remarked to the General that "I wouldn't have missed this for anything." Longstreet was seated at the top of a snake fence at the edge of the woods (Spangler Woods), and looking perfectly calm and imperturbed. He replied, laughing, "The devil you wouldn't! I would like to have missed it very much; we've attacked and been repulsed: look there!"

For the first time I then had a view of the open space between the two positions, and saw it covered with Confederates slowly and sulkily returning towards us in small broken parties, under a heavy fire of artillery. But the fire where we were was not so bad as further to the rear; for although the air seemed alive with shells, yet the greater number burst behind us. The General told me that

Pickett's Division had succeeded in carrying the enemy's position and captured his guns, but after remaining there twenty minutes, it had been forced to retire on the retreat of Heth and Pettigrew on his left. . . .

Major Walton was the only officer with him (Longstreet) when I came up—all the rest had been put in charge. In a few minutes Major Latrobe arrived on foot, carrying his saddle, having just had his horse killed. Colonel Sorrell was also in the same predicament, and Captain Goree's horse was wounded in the mouth. . . .

Soon after I joined General Lee, who had in the meanwhile come to that part of the field on becoming aware of the disaster. If Longstreet's conduct was admirable, that of General Lee was perfectly sublime. He was engaged in rallying and in encouraging the broken troops, and was riding about a little in front of the woods, quite alone, the whole of his staff being engaged in a similar manner further to the rear. His face, which is always placid and cheerful, did not show signs of the slightest disappointment, of annoyance; and he was addressing to every soldier he met a few words of encouragement, such as, "All this will come right in the end: we'll talk it over afterwards; but, in the meantime, all good men must rally. We want all good and true men just now." He spoke to all the wounded men that passed him, and the slightly wounded he exhorted "to bind up their hurts and take up a musket" in this emergency. Very few failed to answer his appeal, and I saw badly wounded men take off their hats and cheer him. He said to me, "This has been a sad day for us, Colonel—a sad day; but we can't expect always to gain victories." He was also kind enough to advise me to get into some more sheltered position as the shells were bursting round us with considerable frequency. . . .

I saw General Wilcox come up to him, and explain, almost crying, the state of his brigade. General Lee immediately shook hands with him and said cheerfully, "Never mind, General, all this has been my fault—it is I that have lost this fight, and you must help me out of it in the best way you can." In this manner I saw General Lee encourage and reanimate his somewhat dispirited troops, and magnanimously take upon his own shoulders the whole weight of the repulse.

5

Retreat to Dixie

By Brigadier General John O. Imboden, C.S.A.

During the Gettysburg campaign, my command—an independent brigade of cavalry—was engaged, by General Lee's confidential orders, in raids on the left flank of his advancing army, destroying railroad bridges and cutting the canal below Cumberland wherever I could, so that I did not reach the field till noon of the last day's battle. I reported direct to General Lee for orders, and was assigned a position to aid in repelling any cavalry demonstration on his rear. None of a serious character being made, my little force took no part in the battle, but were merely spectators of the scene, which transcended in grandeur any that I beheld in any other battle of the war.

When night closed the struggle, Lee's army was repulsed. We all knew that the day had gone against us, but the full extent of the disaster was only known in higher quarters. The carnage of the day was generally understood to have been frightful, yet our army was not in retreat, and it was surmised in camp that with tomorrow's dawn would come a renewal of the struggle. All felt and appreciated the momentous consequences to the cause of Southern independence of final defeat or victory on that great field.

It was a warm summer's night; there were few campfires, and the weary soldiers were lying in groups on the luxuriant grass of the beautiful meadows, discussing the events of the day, speculating on the morrow, or watching that our horses did not straggle off while browsing. About 11 o'clock a horseman came to summon me to General Lee. I promptly mounted and, accompanied by Lieutenant George W. McPhail, an aide on my staff, and guided by the courier who brought the message, rode about two miles toward Gettysburg to where half a dozen small tents were pointed out, a little way from the roadside to our left, as General Lee's headquarters for the night. On inquiry I found that he was not there, but had gone to the headquarters of General A. P. Hill, about half a mile nearer to Gettysburg. When we reached the place indicated, a single flickering candle, visible from the road through the open front of a common wall tent exposed to view Generals Lee and Hill seated on camp stools with a map spread upon their knees. Dismounting, I approached on foot. After exchanging the ordinary salutations General Lee directed me to go back to his headquarters and wait for him. I did so, but he did not make his appearance until about 1 o'clock, when he came riding alone, at a slow walk, and evidently wrapped in profound thought.

When he arrived, there was not even a sentinel on duty at his tent, and no one of his staff was awake. The moon was high in the clear sky and the silent scene was unusually vivid. As he approached and saw us lying on the grass under a tree, he spoke, reined in his jaded horse, and essayed to

dismount. The effort to do so betrayed so much physical
exhaustion that I hurriedly rose and stepped forward to
assist him, but before I reached his side he had succeeded
in alighting, and threw his arm across the saddle to rest,
and fixing his eyes upon the ground leaned in silence and
almost motionless upon his equally weary horse—the two
forming a striking and never-to-be-forgotten group. The
moon shone full upon his massive features and revealed
an expression of sadness that I had never before seen upon
his face. Awed by his appearance I waited for him to speak
until the silence became embarrassing, when, to break it
and change the silent current of his thoughts, I ventured
to remark, in a sympathetic tone, and in allusion to his
great fatigue:

"General, this has been a hard day on you."

He looked up, and replied mournfully:

"Yes, it has been a sad, sad day to us," and immediately
relapsed into his thoughtful mood and attitude. Being unwilling again to intrude upon his reflections, I said no
more. After perhaps a minute or two, he suddenly straight-
ened up to his full height, and turning to me with more
animation and excitement of manner than I had ever seen
in him before, for he was a man of wonderful equanimity,
he said in a voice tremulous with emotion:

"I never saw troops behave more magnificently than
Pickett's division of Virginians did today in that grand
charge upon the enemy. And if they had been supported
as they were to have been—but, for some reason not yet
fully explained to me, were not—we would have held the
position and the day would have been ours." After a moment's pause he added in a loud voice, in a tone almost
of agony, "Too bad! Too bad! OH! TOO BAD!"

I shall never forget his language, his manner, and his

appearance of mental suffering. In a few moments all emotion was suppressed, and he spoke feelingly of several of his fallen trusted officers; among others of Brigadier Generals Armistead, Garnett, and Kemper of Pickett's division. He invited me into his tent, and as soon as we were seated he remarked:

"We must now return to Virginia. As many of our poor wounded as possible must be taken home. I have sent for you, because your men and horses are fresh and in good condition, to guard and conduct our train back to Virginia. The duty will be arduous, responsible, and dangerous, for I am afraid you will be harassed by the enemy's cavalry. How many men have you?"

"About 2,100 effective present, and all well mounted, including McClanahan's six-gun battery of horse artillery."

"I can spare you as much artillery as you require," he said, "but no other troops, as I shall need all I have to return safely by a different and shorter route than yours. The batteries are generally short of ammunition, but you will probably meet a supply I have ordered from Winchester to Williamsport. Nearly all the transportation and the care of all the wounded will be intrusted to you. You will recross the mountain by the Chambersburg Road, and then proceed to Williamsport by any route you deem best, and without a halt till you reach the river. Rest there long enough to feed your animals; then ford the river, and do not halt again till you reach Winchester, where I will again communicate with you."

Shortly after noon of the 4th the very windows of heaven seemed to have opened. The rain fell in blinding sheets; the meadows were soon overflowed, and fences gave way before the raging streams. During the storm, wagons, ambulances, and artillery carriages by hundreds—nay, by thousands—were assembling in the fields along the road from Gettysburg to Cashtown, in one confused and apparently inextricable mass. As the afternoon wore on there was no abatement in the storm. Canvas was no protection against its fury, and the wounded men lying upon the naked boards of the wagonbodies were drenched. Horses and mules were blinded and maddened by the wind and water, and became almost unmanageable. The deafening roar of the mingled sounds of heaven and earth all around us made it almost impossible to communicate orders, and equally difficult to execute them.

About 4 P.M. the head of the column was put in motion near Cashtown, and began the ascent of the mountain in the direction of Chambersburg. I remained at Cashtown giving directions and putting in detachments of guns and troops at what I estimated to be intervals of a quarter or a third of a mile. It was found from the position of the head of the column west of the mountain at dawn of the 5th—the hour at which Young's cavalry and Hart's battery began the ascent of the mountain near Cashtown—that the entire column was 17 miles long when drawn out on the road and put in motion.

After dark I set out from Cashtown to gain the head of the column during the night. My orders had been peremptory that there should be no halt for any cause whatever. If an accident should happen to any vehicle, it was immediately to be put out of the road and abandoned. The column moved rapidly, considering the rough roads and the darkness, and from almost every wagon for miles issued heartrending wails of agony. For four hours I hurried forward on my way to the front, and in all that time I was never out of hearing of the groans and cries of the wounded and dying. Scarcely one in a hundred had received adequate surgical aid, owing to the demands on the hard-working surgeons from still worse cases that had to be left behind. Many of the wounded in the wagons had been without food for 36 hours. Their torn and bloody clothing, matted and hardened was rasping the tender, inflamed, and still oozing wounds. Very few of the wagons had even a layer of straw in them, and all were without springs. The road was rough and rocky from the heavy washings of the preceding day. The jolting was enough to have killed strong men, if long exposed to it. From nearly every wagon as the teams trotted on, urged by whip and shout, came such cries and shrieks as these:

"O God! Why can't I die?"

"Stop! Oh! For God's sake, stop just for one minute; take me out and leave me to die on the roadside."

"I am dying! I am dying! My poor wife, my dear children, what will become of you?"

During this one night I realized more of the horrors of war than I had in all the two preceding years.

And yet in the darkness was our safety, for no enemy would dare attack where he could not distinguish friend from foe. We knew that when day broke upon us we should be harassed by bands of cavalry hanging on our flanks. Therefore our aim was to go as far as possible under cover of the night. Instead of going through Chambersburg, I decided to leave the main road near Fairfield after crossing the mountains, and take "a near cut"* across the country to Greencastle, where daybreak on the morning of the 5th of July found the head of our column. We were now twelve or fifteen miles from the Potomac at Williamsport, our point of crossing into Virginia.

---

* The "Pine Stump" Road through Walnut Bottom, New Fuilford, and Marion.

Here our apprehended troubles began. After the advance—the 18th Virginia Cavalry—had passed perhaps a mile beyond the town, the citizens to the number of thirty or forty attacked the train with axes, cutting the spokes out of ten or a dozen wheels and dropping the wagons in the streets. The moment I heard of it I sent back a detachment of cavalry to capture every citizen who had been engaged in this work, and treat them as prisoners of war. This stopped the trouble there, but the Union cavalry began to swarm down upon us from the fields and crossroads, making their attacks in small bodies, and striking the column where there were few or no guards, and thus creating great confusion.

Our situation was frightful. We had probably 10,000 animals and nearly all the wagons of General Lee's army under our charge, and all the wounded, to the number of several thousand, that could be brought from Gettysburg. Our supply of provisions consisted of a few wagon-loads of flour in my own brigade train, a small lot of fine fat cattle which I had collected in Pennsylvania on my way to Gettysburg, and some sugar and coffee procured in the same way at Mercersburg.

The town of Williamsport is located in the lower angle formed by the Potomac with Conocheague Creek. These streams inclose the town on two sides, and back of it about one mile there is a low range of hills that is crossed by four roads converging at the town. The first is the Greencastle Road leading down the creek valley; next the Hagerstown Road; then the Boonsboro' Road; and lastly the River Road.

Early on the morning of the 6th I received intelligence of the approach from Frederick of a large body of cavalry with three full batteries of six rifled guns. These were the divisions of Generals Buford and Kilpatrick, and Huey's brigade of Gregg's division, consisting, as I afterward learned, of 23 regiments of cavalry, and 18 guns, a total force of about 7,000 men.

I immediately posted my guns on the hills that concealed the town, dismounted my own command to support them, and ordered as many of the wagoners to be formed as could be armed with the guns of the wounded that we had brought from Gettysburg. In this I was greatly aided by Colonel J. L. Black of South Carolina, Captain J. F. Hart commanding a battery from the same state, Colonel William R. Aylett of Virginia, and other wounded officers. By noon about 700 wagoners were organized into companies of 100 each and officered by wounded line officers and commissaries and quartermasters—about 250 of these were given Colonel Aylett on the right next the river— about as many under Colonel Black on the left, and the residue were used as skirmishers. My own command proper was held well in hand in the center.

The enemy appeared in our front about half-past one o'clock on both the Hagerstown and Boonsboro' roads, and the fight began. Every man under my command understood that if we did not repulse the enemy we should all be captured and General Lee's army be ruined by the loss of its transportaion, which at that period could not have been replaced in the Confederacy. The fight began with artillery on both sides. The firing from our side was very rapid, and seemed to make the enemy hesitate about advancing. In a half hour J. D. Moore's battery ran out of ammunition, but as an ordinance train had arrived from Winchester, two wagon-loads of ammunition were ferried across the river and run upon the field behind the guns, and the boxes tumbled out, to be broken open with axes. With this fresh supply our guns were all soon in full play again. As the enemy could not see the supports of our batteries from the hill-tops, I moved the whole line forward to his full view, in single ranks, to show a long front on the Hagerstown approach. My line passed our guns 50 or 100 yards, where they were halted awhile, and then were withdrawn behind the hill-top again, slowly and steadily.

Night was now rapidly approaching, when a messenger from Fitzhugh Lee arrived to urge me to "hold my own," as he would be up in a half hour with 3,000 fresh men. The news was sent along our whole line, and was received with a wild and exultant yell. We knew then that the field was won, and slowly pressed forward. Almost at the same moment we heard distant guns on the enemy's rear and right on the Hagerstown Road. They were Stuart's who was approaching on that road, while Fitzhugh Lee was coming on the Greencastle Road. That settled the contest. The enemy broke to the left and fled by the Boonsboro' Road. It was too dark to follow. When General Fitzhugh Lee joined me with his staff on the field, one of the enemy's shells came near striking him. General Lee thought it came from Eshleman's battery, till, a moment later, he saw a blaze from its gun streaming away from us.

We captured about 125 of the enemy who failed to reach their horses. I could never ascertain the loss on either side. I estimated ours at about 125. The wagoners fought so well that this came to be known as "the wagoners' fight." Quite a number of them were killed in storming a farm from which sharpshooters were rapidly picking off Eshleman's men and horses.

My whole force engaged, wagoners included, did not exceed 3,000 men. The ruse practiced by showing a formidable line on the left, then withdrawing it to fight on the right, together with our numberous artillery, led to the belief that our force was much greater.

By extraordinary good fortune we had thus saved all of General Lee's trains. A bold charge at any time before sunset would have broken our feeble lines, and then we should all have fallen an easy prey to the Federals. The next day our army arrived from Gettysburg.

6

Comparative Losses

The terrible carnage of those three days in the limited battle amphitheater exceeded any blood-letting ever to transpire on American soil. It was an engagement of citizen soldiers possessing varying degree of trained competence. Of the 170,000 involved, more than 50,000 were casualties—killed, wounded, missing or taken prisoner—approximately 30 per cent of the participants.

Official Federal and Confederate records do not conform. The Adjutant General's office lists the names of 12,227 wounded and unwounded Confederates captured July 1-5, whereas the corresponding Confederate figure is 5,000.

	Federal	Confederate	Total
Killed	3,072*	2,592**	5,664
Wounded	14,497*	12,709**	27,206
Missing or captured	5,434*	12,227*	17,661
	23,003	27,528	50,531

* Federal figure
** Confederate figure

7

Speculation

It has been stated and reiterated, "Gettysburg had everything"—the magnitude of the armies, the terrain, the aspect of collision, the closeness of the vicious conflict, and, most of all, the speculation of what might have happened had things been planned and executed in a different manner. Difference of opinion and second guessing occurred as the battle progressed; it persisted as the Army of Virginia retreated to home soil, it will continue—ad infinitum.

What would have been the outcome at Gettysburg had Major General J. E. B. Stuart and his vaunted 10,000, "the eyes and ears of Lee's army," been available prior to and during the entire three-day battle?

The Confederates were converging in force upon Gettysburg from Chambersburg, Carlisle and Harrisburg more rapidly than was the case with the units of the Army of the Potomac fanning out from Frederick along the roads to the north; however, neither Lee or Meade had a knowledge of the location of the enemy.

Brigadier General John Buford's cavalry followed by the infantry corps of Major General John Reynolds and Major General Oliver O. Howard arrived in Gettysburg on June 30h and drove out of town a few Confederates who were in search of shoes and other needed supplies. That night Buford's 4,000 settled on McPherson's Ridge, straddling the Chambersburg Pike, just west of town. The collision occurred shortly after daybreak of July 1 when Major General Henry Heath's Confederate division of Hill's corps ran headlong into the Federal cavalry to start the battle of Gettysburg.

Buford, strengthened by infantry, delayed the Confederate advance from the Cashtown Pass to Gettysburg. The scene then changed for Buford to the Harrisburg Pike, where the same division denied the advance units of Lieutenant General Richard S. Ewell's corps the right of way to Gettysburg. Both stellar delaying actions against vastly superior forces provided the necessary time for Meade to mass troops and form the "Fish Hook" defense, anchored on the south by Round Top and the northeast by Culp's Hill. It was a case of the combination of mobility and firepower delaying the advance of superior forces.

Had this action not occurred, where would the major battle have taken place?

What would have been the effect on the battle had the ailing Ewell driven on during the afternoon of July 1, 1863 to exploit early Confederate successes and to utilize his superior force in the capture of Culps Hill, strategic command post of the Baltimore road and the northeast anchor of the Federal "Fish Hook," before sufficient Union forces were massed to make it secure? He was a successor in command to Lieutenant General Thomas Jackson, accidentally mortally wounded by his own men at Chancellorsville. Had "Stonewall" been in command, what would have transpired?

The following were the words of General Lee showing what his battle plans were for the second day at Gettysburg: "General Longstreet was directed to place the divisions of McLaws and Hood on the right of Hill, partially enveloping the enemy's left, which he was to drive in. General Hill was ordered to threaten the enemy's center to prevent rienforcements being drawn to either wing and cooperate with his right division in Longstreet's attack. General Ewell was instructed to make a simultaneous demonstration upon the enemy's right to be converted into a real attack should opportunity offer." (*Official Records*: vol. 27, part 2, page 319.)

Longstreet had been ordered by Lee on the night of the first to attack as early as practicable on the morning of the second whereupon Longstreet attempted to prevail upon his commander to skirt Round Top to the south, then conduct a defensive campaign. The next day Longstreet temporized until a subordinate division commander, Major General Lafayette McLaws, was directed by Lee to organize and launch the attack, which proceeded at 4 P.M.

The Army of Virginia was better concentrated on the morning of the second than was the case with the Army of the Potomac. Both Little Round Top and Big Round Top, which flanked the Federal line on Cemetery Ridge, were unoccupied until the afternoon. Two of Meade's corps did not arrive until after noontime.

Did this obstinance on the part of the sulking Longstreet make victory impossible?

How would the battle have terminated had Federal Brigadier General Gouverneur K. Warren not discovered that strategic Little Round Top, southern extremity of the "Fish Hook," was unoccupied; and his quick action made possible the repulse of Major General J. S. Hood's Texans?

On that second day, Major General Daniel E. Sickles, without approval of Meade, advanced about one mile to Sherfy's Peach Orchard, producing a wedge vulnerable to attack from three directions, which protruded from the Federal "Fish Hook." Thus the left flank of the Army of the Potomac was exposed. Driven from the Peach Orchard by Longstreet's Confederate attack, fighting raged along the one mile western flank encompassing the rocks of Devil's Den and the slopes of Little Round Top. On the eastern flank, it carried across the Emmitsburg Road to the crest of Cemetery Ridge. With the Confederates converging on the famous Wheat Field from various directions, the 50 acre tract became a bloody "whirl pool." The Federals dropped back to Cemetery Ridge as a retreating army, not an organized fighting force and Brigadier General A. R. Wright temporarily effected a Confederate lodgment on the Ridge. Darkness put an end to the fighting. Had this action been supported, would the Confederates have held Cemetery Ridge and ultimately won the battle of Gettysburg?

The Confederate surge of the third day, Major General George E. Pickett's massive charge, aimed at the midsection of the "Fish Hook," carried across the Emmitsburg Road and for brief minutes to the crest of Cemetery Ridge. This is generally regarded as "the high-water mark of the

Confederacy." The attack repulsed by the Federals, the Confederates walked off the field just before nightfall to set themselves on Seminary Ridge for the expected counter-attack, which never developed. Each side suffered heavy losses—approximately equal. Did the awaiting men in grey hope for an attack by those in blue? Was the battle a clear-cut victory and loss?

The men of Pickett's, Heth's, Pender's and Anderson's divisions, which took part in the attack totaled 14,000. Lee's instructions were that some 25,000 troops should be employed in a coordinated attack on the enemy's left and center. Would the charge as planned have succeeded in capturing Cemetery Ridge?

A brigade commander in the Confederate army at Gettysburg, General John B. Gordon, wrote the following in *Reminiscences of the Civil War*:

It now seems certain that impartial military critics, after thorough investigation, will consider the following as established:

First: That General Lee distinctly ordered Longstreet to attack early the morning of the second day, and if he had done so, two of the largest corps of Meade's army would not have been in the fight. But Longstreet delayed the attack until four o'clock in the afternoon, and thus lost his opportunity of occupying Little Round Top, the key to the position, which he might have done in the morning without firing a shot or losing a man.

Second: That General Lee ordered Longstreet to attack at daybreak on the morning of the third day, and that he did not attack until two or three o'clock in the afternoon, the artillery opening at one.

Third: That General Lee, according to the testimony

of Colonel Walter Taylor, Colonel C. S. Venable and General A. L. Long, who were present when the order was given ordered Longstreet to make the attack on the last day with the three divisions of his corps and two divisions of A. P. Hill's corps, and that instead of doing so he sent 14,000 men to assail Meade's army in his strong position and heavily intrenched.

Fourth: That the great mistake of the halt on the first day would have been repaired on the second, and even on the third day, if Lee's orders had been vigorously executed, and that General Lee died believing (the testimony on this point is overwhelming) that he lost Gettysburg at last by Longstreet's disobedience of orders."

On the evening of July 3rd Lee stated before Pickett and Longstreet: "This was all my fault, General Pickett. This has been my fight and the blame is mine. Your men did all men can do. The fault is entirely my own." Had the Longstreet plan of battle been pursued, what then?

The Army of Northern Virginia, 50,000 strong, deserted the battle amphitheater the night of Saturday, July 4th, retracing its steps toward home soil. Lee had given up hope of dislodging Meade from his strong position, and the latter did not choose to launch a counterattack on wooded Seminary Ridge. That same day news was received that Vicksburg, in the "West," had fallen to Major General U. S. Grant.

The Potomac was in flood stage and the Confederate-constructed pontoon bridge had been washed away. For nine days the army, short of supplies, was forced to bivouac in the mud as the torrent subsided. Could a concentrated Federal offense of the force of 80,000 available men have destroyed the Army of Northern Virginia and ended the war on the banks of the swollen Potomac—a war which was to last two more long, weary years?

Did the defensive-minded Meade want offensive-minded Lee to escape, or were there other reasons why a Federal attack was not launched?

Was Gettysburg, in so far as outcome is concerned, the closest major battle ever waged?

Had the Confederacy emerged victorious at Gettysburg, as had been the case at First Manassas, the Peninsula, the battles near Richmond, the Shenandoah Valley campaigns, Second Manassas, Fredericksburg and Chancellorsville, and had invasion of the North continued, would England and France have intervened to institute an independent nation in the South to supply the Old World with raw cotton?

The Battle of Gettysburg was the start of a steady flow of Spencer repeating carbines and Sharps breech-loading rifles from the Federal Ordnance Department. Was there any way the Confederacy could cope with this tremendous increase in firepower in the hands of the invader?

Epilogue

On July 14, 1863 Lincoln wrote the following to General Meade, but he decided not to sign and send it: "I do not believe you appreciate the magnitude of the misfortune involved in Lee's escape. He was within your grasp, and to have closed upon him would, in connection with our other late successes, have ended the war . . . Your golden opportunity is gone, and I am disturbed immeasurable because of it. I beg you will not consider this a prossecution, or persecution of yourself. As you had learned that I was dissatisfied, I have thought it best to kindly tell you why."

At a later time Lincoln, in reference to Meade, reminded Simon Cameron, "Why should we censure a man who has done so much for his Country because he did not do a little more?"

Index

086448